The intimacy of
Death
and
Dying

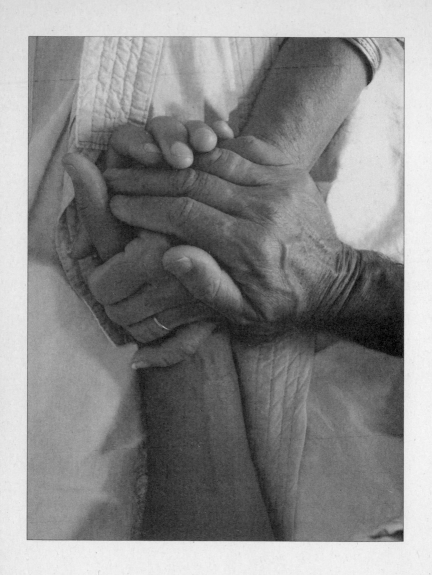

The *intimacy of* Death *and* Dying

SIMPLE GUIDANCE
TO HELP YOU THROUGH

Claire Leimbach, Trypheyna McShane,
Zenith Virago

inspired LIVING

ALLEN&UNWIN

Photo acknowledgements
Pages ii, 37, 52, 64, 77, 193 *Claire Leimbach*
Page 28 *Kayo Jeandel*
Pages 98, 174, 215, 239 *Jeff Dawson*
Pages 128, 151 *Trypheyna McShane*
Page 250 *Merilee Bennett*

First published in 2009

Inspired Living, an imprint of
Allen & Unwin
83 Alexander Street
Crows Nest NSW 2065
Australia
Phone: (61 2) 8425 0100
Fax: (61 2) 9906 2218
Email: info@allenandunwin.com
Web: www.allenandunwin.com

Cataloguing-in-Publication details are available
from the National Library of Australia
www.librariesaustralia.nla.gov.au

ISBN 978 1 74175 894 8

Internal design by Mathematics
Flower illustrations by Trypheyna McShane
Set in 10/14 pt Sabon by Midland Typesetters, Australia
Printed in Australia by McPherson's Printing Group

10 9 8 7 6 5 4 3 2 1

In gratitude
to
Trish, John and Sylvia
and all who have gone before to light the way

Birth and death are only doors through which we pass,
sacred thresholds on our journey.

Birth and death are a game of hide-and-seek.

So laugh with me, hold my hand,
let us say good-bye, say good-bye, to meet again soon.

Thich Nhat Hanh

Contents

Foreword

Not so very long ago, when I reached my 78th birthday, I was lying back luxuriating in the thought that I was still only getting older when, as if I had been given an electric shock, I suddenly realised that I wasn't just getting older, I was old.

'Old, old, old', my daughter Georgia had written in a poem when she was about five years of age. 'His hands were wivvered and trembling with cold.' I looked down at my hands. They weren't yet 'wivvered' and, as it was summer, there wasn't much chance of them dropping off with cold. I leaped out of bed, feeling young, young, young, (not true, but I did creak my way out of bed).

Later, I realised this had been an important awakening. A jump from acknowledging that I was old, into a place where I was suddenly and vividly embracing my own mortality. It may sound strange that I'd hidden this reckoning for so long. It wasn't that I was fearful of death, nor that I had surrendered myself to cosmetic surgery, but I think I had been so active and alert in my daily life that this was where I had chosen to spend most of my being.

The majority of us are brought up with all manner of notions about age and dying. 'Death comes to everyone', 'death is all in the mind' or, 'do not go gentle into that good night ... rage, rage, rage against the dying of the light.' And one that I particularly like, by Woody Allen: 'It's not that I'm afraid to die. I just don't want to be there when it happens.'

Dr Irvin Yalom reminds us in his book, *Staring at the Sun*, that death may come slowly or it may come swiftly, depriving us of the ability to say goodbye. It is not something we can schedule or control. 'Death comes to us whether we're prepared or not, sometimes stretching us to the limits of our endurance, refusing to allow us to avoid it, or fix it.'

Another reality is that none of us has any idea of how or when we shall die. Those who have a serious illness might have a notion of how, but still can't be sure of when. Even more certain is that we can't know how we shall behave. I think I shall be calm and accepting, but I might turn out to be a screaming banshee. Who knows? Which is why death is such a mysterious encounter for all of us, irrespective of faith or lack of faith.

All of us hope for death without pain. Most would like those we love to be there, with us and for us. We probably would not choose to linger. And for those who are watching over the dead and dying, we want to move bravely through our grief. We want funeral arrangements to be smooth. The mystical and practical to come together with love, tenderness and humour.

Nobody told me that death does not remove a person from life. When I wrote about the death of my elder son Jonathan who had wrestled with schizophrenia for seven fierce years, I was able to discover that there had been meaning within the tortuous journey that was Jonathan's life. The meaning was life itself, with all its paradoxes, its joy and its pain, its weakness and its strength, its anger and its love. Perhaps experiences of death happen at times of intense grief or joy. Perhaps at these moments, our subconscious minds are able to break through the confines of everyday life, and remind us we are part of a much bigger existence, one that has no boundaries.

'Grief never leaves you,' I once heard writer V.S. Naipaul say, 'but it mutates into a deepening awareness of the greater capacity for love, and an extraordinary awareness of the interconnectedness of life.'

That is why this book, *The Intimacy of Death and Dying*, fills such a comforting hollow in the uncertainty of our lives. It tells us how to plump the pillows, how to speak to death, what it might bring to us, who shall be invited to the last supper, and how. It makes death seem familiar, something we can accept, be practical about, be frightened, find strength through friends. The stories in this book are brave and honest. The authors have been generous with their thoughts and experiences. They write of the luminescence of death and its sometime wretchedness. They bring us to the bedsides of families and friends. I read with gratitude.

Anne Deveson AO

Preface

Death and dying unite us in a common humanity. There are many books on the subject, but few speak to us from the heart. They don't express how deeply personal the experience is of having someone die—nor the uniqueness of every journey. We don't talk much about death either, so we don't have a rich resource to draw on, to support us in finding our own way through this life-changing process. Without awareness of these potentials it's hard for people to express everything they hold in their hearts, and to find the gifts amongst the sadness, bewilderment and pain.

There's something very liberating when we share with each other the profound stories of our lives. This was a vital element for us in writing this book. We wanted it to be real, to be human, and to provide stepping-stones for others facing the care of someone who is dying, and support them in finding their own way to honour a loved one who has died. That's why *The Intimacy of Death and Dying* presents so many personal stories of the journeys others have taken. We wanted readers to have information that was tangible, to gain real comfort from knowing others have faced terminal illness, the death of a child, lingering death, accidents, suicide and many other situations around death.

We also wanted to give people as much information as possible because death offers us so many opportunities, to reassess who we are and what we want from our own lives, to care for someone we love, to make last wishes come true, to be creative, to find laughter in the midst of sadness and to celebrate life. The book is filled with simple, practical advice on everything from caring for loved ones at home and what you might expect if someone chooses to die in hospital, to dealing with paperwork and organising a funeral. Dozens of suggestions are made on how to make the remaining time with a loved one truly special, how to keep them comfortable and nurtured, and the wonderful opportunities available for celebrating their life once they are gone.

The many personal stories also help readers understand the intimate landscape of death and dying—from bewilderment and sometimes paralysing fear, to unexpected miracles and humour even in the face of terrible tragedy. Our commitment to conveying the gifts that come with death and dying is born of many years' experience, and we believe by embracing death we are able to live life more fully.

Talking about death

There's no rehearsal for death; that's what can make it so challenging—that and the fact that death often meets us unexpectedly when we are least prepared to face such loss. It is not something we can schedule or control.

Death is a journey we all have to take sooner or later. It's possibly the biggest journey we will ever take. So why would we not want to explore the nuances of death, as it also offers us many gifts?

A good death is possible, a good funeral is crucial, not so much for the person who has died, but for the bereaved. Preparation, consideration and open dialogue with family and friends are essential elements of both, and they go a long way in making the entire experience one that is easier to bear, more meaningful and appropriate, and even one that offers us useful and sometimes deeply rewarding insights.

Not everything about death is sad and scary. There can be moments of intense love, supreme happiness, unexpected kindness, even laughter. The stories and guidance we offer allow you the chance to explore the rich landscape of death and dying, so that you too can discover what we have learnt and are still learning—that death offers us far more than we might imagine.

Every death is uniquely different, just as we are as individuals. In sharing their experiences, these storytellers hope to encourage a deeper insight into life and living through being prepared to embrace death and dying.

The more conscious we can be, the better we will deal with our process of loss and grief. It may still be painful, but we will be able to be with ourselves and each other in a more understanding and compassionate way.

As we set out on our journey together, we want to share with you what we have learnt during the many years we have spent with those who are dying. We have included guidance, because there are lots of considerations and decisions to be made while caring for a loved one, and after they are gone. Seeing how others handled the detail can help take the pressure off you. It can also spark your own creative ways of handling the situation you face. The important thing is to take what feels right and useful, for you know in your heart what your loved one and you most need.

We have often been asked: Who is this book for? This book is for everyone.

Losing my mother to cancer

The day after my father's sudden death I was helping my mum, Fran, to dress in their bedroom. The furniture was still out of place from the paramedics being there. Mum looked up at the phone, blaming herself for not having rung the ambulance immediately. Instead, she had rung neighbours for help. It was a massive and sudden stroke that killed him. No-one had been prepared for this.

There was a vacant disbelief that Dad would never lie on his side of the bed again. His bedside drawers still held the loose coins from his pockets. His shoes and thick, woollen work socks lay near his wardrobe. You could smell him in the air. His pillow held a vague Brylcreem scent, clothes evidence of his work in the garden. There was an expectant feeling that he would be back from the bathroom any moment. That I would hear his deep voice, bellowing laugh and limping rhythmic gait coming up the long hallway.

I helped Mum lift her arm through her shirt sleeve. Her right arm. The one with nerve damage and swelling from a period of radiotherapy twenty years before. I noticed two large, weeping sores on her upper arm that needed dressing. I asked Mum what they were.

'Oh Maggie, don't worry, they're just tumours.'

'What do you mean?' I said. 'Where did they come from?'

'Well, the breast cancer has come back again.'

From that day onwards, Mum did not spend a single night on her own and the four of us children cared for her. When we were to bury Dad, Mum had bought a double plot in the lawn cemetery. It never crossed my mind that she might be joining him so soon.

My parents had married in the 1950s and been together for 40 years. In the early 1960s my mother developed breast cancer. It responded well to radiotherapy. No-one in the family was aware of the life-threatening nature of Mum's illness. Remarkably, her extraordinary remission lasted 25 years.

In stark contrast to my father's death, Mum's was slow and expected. Now, despite being the youngest, I took on a special role in the family: I was the one the oncologist told about Mum's shortened life expectancy, which had suddenly been reduced from two years to a matter of months. He explained that chemotherapy would not cure Mum's cancer but might ease her suffering and extend her life a little. With this treatment, she was expected to live for another nine months; without treatment, her life expectancy could be as short as three months. I was horrified. I asked the oncologist if Mum knew this. 'She never asked me,' was his response.

I could see how sick Mum was from the chemo and felt that she probably wouldn't continue the treatment if she knew the full story. Lying beside her on her bed the next morning, I asked her if she wanted to know what the doctor had said.

'Of course I want to know. What did he say?'

'He said you are not going to get better. You may only have months to live.' I burst into uncontrollable tears. Putting my arms around her I said, 'I am really going to miss you.'

'Well, I expect you will Maggie,' she replied, smiling at me. It was as if she knew all this already.

From that day she stopped her chemotherapy. We celebrated by going to lunch, even though she struggled to reacquaint herself with the taste of food.

Breaking the news to my sister, the oldest in the family, wasn't easy. We all realised that this was a time to pack in precious memories and experiences.

I worked hard for the remaining months of that year to complete my PhD, which I had struggled on for years, submitting my thesis three days before Christmas. My father would never see it, so I wrapped a bound copy and handed it to Mum as a Christmas present.

This first Christmas without Dad and the last with Mum was bittersweet. At Mum's request, we all gathered at my brother's place rather than at our family home.

Between us, Mum and I had made cushion covers as a gift for my brother. Knowing how hard it now was for Mum to sew, he broke down in tears as he unwrapped the parcels. It was a project Mum and I loved doing together. We chose the fabrics to go with my brother's lounge. I cut them. Mum used her one good hand to guide them through the sewing machine. To finish them, I followed her instructions exactly. While on the surface it was about focusing on the gift, it allowed us to relive the days of her teaching me to sew.

Mum's birthday was two days after Christmas, and her birthdays and Christmases often merged. She wasn't used to separate birthday celebrations. This time, however, the family rang everyone in Mum's address book and invited them around for afternoon tea. We organised sandwiches and a beautiful birthday cake. Most of her friends knew she was ill and not going to get better so the house was full of people. At the age of 75, she had her first and only surprise birthday party. The place was abuzz with stories and laughter—it was like a wake of sorts, but with Mum there. She was in great spirits.

Mum's real fear about dying was being in pain. As it was her express wish to die at home—the home where she had raised her children, and where she and my father had spent most of their lives—we discussed my looking after her to monitor the pain relief. Although I am a nurse and midwife it had been a long time since I practised. I remember feeling an overwhelming responsibility to help my mum on her journey towards a beautiful death, in much the same way as I had assisted at many homebirths. She trusted me to help her through. To take on this role I needed the support of my brothers and sister.

We had a clear understanding that Mum was to call me as soon as she reached the stage where she needed nursing and I would return home. A few weeks later, I got that call. Mum was not able to eat and was experiencing pain. I flew to her the next day. She had a very supportive family doctor who made home visits and linked her into the palliative care team. Within a week we had a huge amount of liquid morphine in the kitchen pantry. My brother and I often wondered what it would taste like.

Mum grew frailer and more exhausted by the day. She was shrinking right before our eyes. My brother grew anxious. He thought Mum should go to a hospice. This was a crisis point for our 'mini hospice at home' and the routine we had established. Wasn't I doing a good job? Did Mum really need care that we couldn't provide? I didn't know what to say, so I asked Mum.

She said she knew she was getting the best possible care at home, better than at a hospice, and she wanted to stay. The question never arose again.

One day the palliative care nurse gave me some invaluable advice. She explained that when Mum died we would need to call the local funeral director, but that once informed they often came immediately. She advised us not to ring them until we were ready, taking as much time as we needed to say goodbye to Mum.

A devout Catholic, Mum was visited by the priest at least once a week and received Holy Communion almost daily from visiting church people. These rituals were really important to her. On one of these visits she asked me to get her pyx, a beautiful, golden, highly decorated container used to carry the hosts for Holy Communion. She gave this to her fellow church worker who gave Mum her last Holy Communion. Mum was showing the first outward signs of letting go, passing on her valued possessions. She also went around the house making a list of what each person was to receive.

One weekend, lying on her bed in the afternoon with her granddaughters around her, she got out all her jewellery and divided the pieces among the girls, including her engagement and eternity rings which she always wore. It was a relief to see her so accepting of death. Over the years I had witnessed many people's anger and inner struggles as they and their families resisted the inevitable.

At night I slept with Mum, on Dad's side of the bed. My sister would sit by Mum's side during the day. We didn't want to suddenly find Mum not breathing. We wanted to know what she was going through, to be there whenever she needed anything, whether it was a few words of conversation or simply to hold her hand.

We organised a wheelchair and commode to make it easier for Mum to go on short outings. The last time she left her bedroom, we were all together in the garden, laughing, enjoying the flowers and fresh air. After that, her room became her world and the centre of our universe. It was peaceful, sacred.

My brother's partner visited often. An accomplished pianist, he played magnificent piano concertos which Mum could hear from her room. He also organised the most fragrant roses to be delivered with rose oil and a burner. It was such a thoughtful gift. As Mum deteriorated, her smell was changing, her body was decaying. The rose perfume filled her room.

As Mum started slipping in and out of consciousness, I went shopping and bought 28 different patterned fabrics to make a quilt in her memory. Many of the pieces were what I remember Mum having worn as a blouse or a skirt. I spent most of my days on the veranda putting the quilt together while my sister sat with Mum. It became a focal point in the house. Everyone visiting would come to see how the quilt was progressing. My sister embroidered Mum's name on the strips of silk that formed the border.

It became progressively harder to bear Mum's slow deterioration. The nights were particularly difficult. I didn't want to sleep, and would sit at Mum's feet, holding them, letting her know I was still there. I would check to be sure she wasn't in pain. She lay there quietly and peacefully.

On the second to last night, at about 3 a.m., I saw something I felt I was not meant to see. Two faces came over Mum's: an old Aboriginal woman's face, then my father's. Their faces appeared to merge with Mum's. I closed my eyes, thinking this was for Mum, not for me.

The next night, Mum's last, the same thing happened. I watched this time, as I thought it must be meant for me to see after all. The faces seemed to be guiding Mum from the physical world to the spirit world. While I felt comforted by this, I was also self-conscious and reluctant to mention it to anyone for fear they would think I was a bit crazy.

She took her last breath at 9.30 a.m. We were all there beside her, touching her. Her face was sunken, as if her spirit had left three days before and her body was just slowly unwinding, and then it stopped. By the time she died, I felt Mum had happily departed to join Dad and her own mother in the spirit world.

My sister and I washed Mum's body, dressing her in a lovely white nightie. From time to time during the day I visited her, lying next to her and talking with her.

We rang friends to tell them the news, inviting them to say their goodbyes. My aunt was very grateful for this opportunity. It helped her to have a lasting memory of a peaceful and beautiful end to the life of a woman filled with kindness and love. This was unusual for many people, who were grateful to see their friend in death at home and not in the cold impersonal surroundings of a funeral home. Fifty years ago, saying goodbye at home would have been entirely normal.

Mum was in the same bed she had slept in since marrying Dad. It was the bed that every one of her children had slept in from time to time. A bed of great comfort.

My cousin came later that night and, finding Mum still in her bed, asked when we were planning to call the funeral director. It dawned on me then that I had to let her go. I packed some clothes she used to wear in winter for outside walking. Her body was cold so I packed a warm woollen cardigan and her walking shoes, symbolising her moving away, travelling far on her own.

I called the funeral director and their people arrived very quickly. I wasn't prepared for the black body bag and asked if they could leave the zip open for Mum's face. We gave Mum a guard of honour as she was carried out to the waiting black van. I cried and cried. It was over. This beautiful death was over.

The quilt was finished in time to drape Mum's timber coffin. She was buried on top of Dad in their double plot purchased only eight months before. I now have Mum's bed as my own bed and hold the quilt in trust until the next family member dies, when their name will be added to the border.

Maggie Haertsch

Embracing death

Even though death is inevitable, and frequently occurs around us, it's astonishing we don't speak more openly about it.

There's so much death can teach us about life. Death has many gifts. It can help us discover the best of ourselves.

It's also a real help to family and friends if you have some idea how would you prefer to die. Would you like someone to be there with you? What would you like to leave behind? Are there precious possessions you would like to pass on? What would you like to be remembered for? Are there things you would like to say or do before you go? Do some relationships need to be healed or sorted out? Would you like to leave letters, videos or a spoken message for those you love?

This is your journey, so don't be afraid to get down to the nitty-gritty. Are you concerned about pain? If so, are there people you need to tell who can help you understand what choices you might have? Do you want to die in your bed at home, or would you prefer to go to hospital? Why not start making a few notes and, if you feel comfortable, discuss with others what you would prefer.

Then, of course, it helps to think about what it will be like for those left behind. Sorting out the practicalities can make all the difference. What are your finances like? Have you made it easy for loved ones to sort out your estate? Have you written a will? Have you thought about an executor, someone who will handle the settlement of your affairs such as gathering together your assets, paying debts, distributing your estate and organising for your body to be dealt with in accordance with your will?

What do you want done with your body? Some people have clear ideas about what they want done, while others aren't sure, so you might want to think about it. Some people favour cremation and having their ashes scattered. What would you like done with your ashes? If you would like to be buried in the earth, what sort of coffin appeals? Where is your body to be placed? Do you want to donate your organs or leave your body to science? If so, make sure you let others know.

Thinking a little about your own death can also help you face the death of those you love. You might like to ask yourself, and your loved ones, what can you do to support them when their moment comes?

Travelling across the world to be with my dying father

My father John died at the age of 83. My sister Roxana, my sister-in-law Imogen and I were all at his bedside and although he was clinically unconscious, I'm sure he knew his girls were around him, something he had always enjoyed.

My relationship with my father had not always been an easy one. When I was a little girl I worshipped him. I was his firstborn and he took me everywhere on his old bicycle. I was born in Yorkshire, as peace was declared in Europe. These were frugal times but there was no shortage of love and my father's strong arms to protect me.

He was larger than life, a 'big' man in every sense. He was an Anglican priest in a rural parish all his working life, with a devoted following. People came from miles around to his services, because he was an extremely eloquent and powerful orator.

As I reached my teenage years, however, he and I had some mighty conflicts, often about my boyfriends who were never good enough for his precious firstborn. I think it is no coincidence that both my sister and I went to live on the other side of the world, in order to forge our own paths in life.

It was with some of these thoughts in mind that I flew to be with him in his last days.

Every day for the week leading up to Pa's death, my sister Roxana and I set off in the morning in brilliant spring sunshine to be with him in the local cottage hospital. The 15-minute drive took us through the sweeping Norfolk landscape, just waking after its winter's sleep. The hedgerows were white with blackthorn blossom and lined with daffodils. All the trees had crisp young leaves bursting out of their otherwise dead-looking branches. The weather was still very cold some days, but everywhere there were the signs of rebirth and the promise of renewal. For me this was a reminder of the endless cycle of birth and death, a metaphor in nature for what I was experiencing.

We would sit with my father all morning, sometimes chatting about daily events in the family, often just quietly being there. In between times, I read *The Tibetan Book of Living and Dying*, whose wisdom and insight gave me great comfort.

He loved the little CD player Roxana brought and, up until the end, listened to the classical music he had always loved, particularly the Gregorian and Russian chants I brought him. He had always had a wonderful baritone voice and had sung a wide range of devotional music, as well as entertaining us with popular songs and his own compositions.

The day after I had arrived Roxana and I took Pa in the car back to our brother Merlin's house, where we all spent the afternoon together in warm spring sunshine. He was surrounded by his family and four of his dearly loved grandchildren. My mother was there and at the end of the day she was able to kiss him goodbye for the last time, a moving scene since, due to a stroke, she was unable to make the journeys into the hospital to see him.

Much of the time he sat in his wheelchair looking over the garden, with its single cherry tree covered in pink blossom. He would drift in and out of consciousness with a peace and serenity I found to be his greatest gift to us.

Every year in my childhood I remember him going away on silent retreats and, although I didn't fully understand these when I was young, it is clear to me now that at the time of his withdrawing from the world as he approached death, he was easily able to drop into a place of inner peace. From things he said over the years, I believe he had a great dread of death, but when the time came he made the journey with grace and surrender. This quiet acceptance was an inspiration to us all.

I found I had no difficulty in letting go of old resentments and angst. I felt I could meet him in the present moment, where neither the past nor the future had a place. In life he had often been frustratingly concerned with appearances, which got in the way of the spontaneity and intimacy of our earlier childhood days. Yet in these last few days all that fell away. We felt closer to him, and I believe he to us, than at any time since we were small children.

Pa clearly outlined what he wanted for his funeral and burial which were to be with minimum fuss. He didn't want a long church service, he said, he was happy to forget about our world. He was even surprised when I asked his advice about winding up the antique clocks, a job he took very seriously and allowed no-one else to do. They are known to run down and refuse to go after their owner dies.

He asked me to go to the churchyard opposite my brother's house and select the spot for his grave. He wanted to be buried like Robert Louis Stevenson:

Under a wide and starry sky, dig the grave and let me lie.
Glad have I lived and gladly die, and I lay me down with a will.

I had sent those words to him the previous year from Samoa where Stevenson died, and they resonated for him.

Every night in the week leading up to his death the comet Hale-Bopp was brilliant in the sky, a phenomenon which only happens every 700 years. It left a spectacular long trail of greenish-white light bursting from its tail. After his death it began to fade, and the weather sank back into a grey winter gloom.

Until the last week Pa remained fiercely independent and insisted on showering himself, although he wasn't really up to it. The nurses all loved him and said what a special man he was, even though it was hard for them to hold back and let him do it all himself.

Thankfully, his kidney failure was relatively pain free. It was not until two days before he died that he needed any morphine and even then my brother Merlin was able to come in at the end of his working day and read T.S. Eliot's *Four Quartets* aloud to him, a poem that had special significance to them both. Even while Pa lay apparently unconscious and close to slipping into the unknown, we trusted that he was nevertheless still able to hear, and so my brother sat down to read the entire poem with all the subtlety and skill that Dad had taught him. The words, with their profound reflections on time and mortality, filled the room and became an intense meditation for all of us.

Towards the end when you are focused only on the breath, every breath can seem an eternity and you are left to wonder how many breaths make up a day. In my family's all-too-busy lives, it was good for me to step off the merry-go-round for a while and appreciate life from an entirely different perspective.

The week before his death was probably the longest of my life. As he got weaker, we were doing all the things you do for a baby and I was reminded of how our parents do these same things for us at birth, and then as their life draws to a close the roles are reversed. It is said that 'our parents see us into the world and we see them out'. I will always remember how much it meant to my father to have his children beside him in those last days. The peaceful acceptance with which he faced his death will always remain his greatest gift. When he finally took his last long breath Roxana, Imogen and I were beside him; sadly, Merlin had already left for work. We stayed at his bedside feeling a deep peace descend. I felt it was as it should be, and there was for me a profound sense of completion.

Pa was always there for those in need and when he died the letters poured in, acknowledging how much he had meant in the lives of so many. He had married, christened and buried several generations.

A few days after he died we had a very small funeral service for the family and the village my parents had grown to love so dearly in the last ten years.

Early on in the day Roxana and I picked armfuls of daffodils from Merlin's garden, along with all kinds of spring blossoms and new leaves from the hedgerows, and took them to my parents' house. We laid them on our huge dining-room table and for the next three hours we made a giant Tahitian lei, like a huge floral necklace. I had first gone to Tahiti more than twenty years before and returned yearly since. This ritual was a very important part of my grieving process and a special personal offering to my father. The lei was in yellow and white, a symbol of spring and rebirth. It was so big it encircled the coffin and took five of us to carry it over to the church. The village had never seen anything like it. Carli, my eldest daughter, said she could imagine her grandfather's head peeking up from behind the flowers.

As I sat in the ancient church, which has seen nine hundred years of worship, I realised I hadn't been to a service since the last one my father took. Suddenly I was engulfed in a wave of childhood memories of him in church. He was always so impressive and his sermons awesome.

The rector had agreed to our choice of gravesite. Miraculously, when they dug, it appeared to have no previous graves under it, a rare thing in a graveyard that had been in continuous use for nine centuries. It was a secluded spot covered with daffodils, beyond the east end of the church, its flint wall surmounted at the eave by a Celtic cross in crumbling stone. We all felt it was a perfect place for this man who understood peace so well.

Claire Leimbach

Choosing burial or cremation

Deciding whether to be buried or cremated is a very personal choice. There are many options, from burial in a small churchyard to being scattered at sea.

For many people it is important they have a particular spot marked as the burial place of a loved one. Visiting the grave with flowers and sitting quietly communing with someone who is gone can be very comforting. There's also a deeply felt need to mark the place where someone has died, in the case of accidental deaths, such as the crosses and flowers seen by the roadside at the site of an accident.

Now families are scattered across the world, many no longer have a particular attachment to any one place, so it may be difficult to choose a burial spot that is meaningful or convenient for everyone in the family to visit.

In many cities, space constraints mean that the price of plots has become so high that they are unaffordable to many; if you do want a city plot it is advisable to make inquiries and buy one well ahead of time.

Earlier generations wouldn't have thought twice about burying their dead on their land. Now it is necessary to get council permission to bury your loved ones on private land.

In New Zealand, Maori *maraes* (traditional meeting houses) generally have a cemetery alongside them. In this way not only the extended family but the tribe rest together. It is also culturally very important that they are buried on their land.

For many indigenous people it is essential they are buried in their country, because they believe all things are part of the web of life, and that their bodies will help to nurture the land which has supported them.

Some large city cemeteries are divided into religious denominations and designed as parks, places as much for the living as those who have passed away. Some families like to stay physically together in death in family vaults or graves. Some have a strong sense of the land where they want to be buried. Others simply want to be with loved ones.

Natural burial grounds are also being established. Here the body is placed in a shroud or eco-friendly coffin, then a tree is planted on top. The sapling is nourished by the body. It in turn supports flora and fauna, so ultimately your loved one's remains become part of a forest of friends. Many natural burial grounds allow benches to be placed nearby so that people can sit, chat, reflect or bring a picnic to be with their loved ones, enjoying the peaceful surroundings. With today's technologies it is feasible to mark the placement of the tree with a GPS system. You can also choose to have a marker, either on the ground or on the tree. The Natural Death centres in Australia and the United Kingdom offer help and guidance. See the websites www.natural deathcentre.org.au and www.naturaldeath.org.uk.

With cremation, there is a different sense of place, unless you decide to bury the ashes in a specially designated area. One mother who lost her teenage son in a car accident took weeks to decide where to bury her son's ashes. After numerous trips to various cemeteries, she realised her main concern was that her son be with people he knew, so she decided to lay him to rest with his grandmother. This gave her great comfort.

If you live in the city and would like to sprinkle the ashes in a park, it's important you consult your local authority. Generally, small informal gatherings do not require permission, but a larger more formal gathering would have to be booked with the park's management.

You might like to think about where you are going to keep the ashes if you are not going to scatter them immediately. Crematoriums offer a range of urns at various prices; just remember that the most expensive is not necessarily proof of your love, any more than is choosing the most expensive coffin. It is what is in your heart that matters. Some people prefer to find or make a more personal container, such as a lovely craft box or pottery urn.

After the funeral there's no pressure to dispose of the ashes immediately. Some people like to wait for a particular anniversary or other date that is meaningful. It's also worth considering keeping some of the ashes of a young parent who has passed away, so that when the mother or father's children are old enough they can do something special with their parent's remains.

One elderly lady couldn't decide what to do with her husband's ashes and didn't feel comfortable having them in the house, but was happy when close friends took care of them for her in the meantime. They placed the ashes in their wine cupboard as the man loved his wine.

Another woman who was a travelling sales person kept her dad's ashes with her in the car for a couple of years, as it helped her to feel close to him.

If you want to keep the ashes long term, that's fine; there are no rules. You may want your loved one's ashes in a container on the mantlepiece or in a special spot in the garden where you can always be reminded of them.

Some people, like Buddhists, have a sense of impermanence. They are not attached to the physical remains of a loved one and find it liberating to scatter them to the four winds or in the ocean. Others like to take some of the ashes and scatter them at special places which had particular significance for that person during life, such as a favourite holiday destination, beach or park.

Island people, fishermen and those whose lives depend on the sea generally want to return to the ocean in death, as do many sailors and surfers and all those who love the ocean and want their ashes scattered there as a symbol of the infinite.

Clearly, in our society we are at a point where we are redefining funerals and the way in which we celebrate the lives of our loved ones and their remains. The options are many, so try to discuss and consider them with family and friends ahead of time.

Making my mother's last summer special

My mother's diagnosis came as a shock to all of us. A woman with a joyous love of life, my mum Jenny discovered she had a serious digestive cancer just before her retirement.

So began the daunting day-to-day path of this new reality.

At the time, two of her adult sons had left the city while Andrew was living with her and I nearby. Our other brother Chris was a regular visitor from the UK.

During her illness there were two periods of remission. The sense of relief was so great. There was a new gratitude for every day as we dared to dream of a life returned to normal. Mum was her true shining self and all of us shared her hope. She was attracting new people into her life, special friends drawn by her positive attitude and spirit. These friends became so important in sharing her final journey, sometimes more so than lifelong friends who couldn't relate to the way Mum saw life now.

As time passed and her symptoms returned, the frailty of her body and the limited time we had left together became clearer. We made the most of the time we had, sharing holidays, special times and simple joys like walking along the beach or having a cuddle. The intermittent chemotherapy would leave her feeling nauseous, tired and stressed, and sometimes burnt her skin from the inside.

Two years later, at the beginning of summer, Mum really wanted to hold on as Chris was flying home. The chemotherapy was becoming too much now. Mum made the difficult, confronting decision to stop the treatment. After this there was no idea of prognosis. Weeks or months, no-one knew.

However, with the chemicals wearing off, Mum sprung back into the joyous being we knew her to be. She looked so sparkly-eyed it was hard to imagine a downward spiral. The only reminder of her illness was the build up of fluid in her abdomen, which caused bloating and discomfort. Every two weeks she would go to hospital to have it drained, up to 5 litres at a time. So although we had lots of picnics and special times and Mum in such good spirits, it was clear she wasn't well. It was sad for her to know she would never experience grandchildren and to see how the illness affected us all. In many ways our lives were on hold. Our commitment was to loving and supporting her and sharing her journey.

The bloating was getting worse and the quality of her life decreasing. Mum's sister, Karin, arrived from overseas and we took our last holiday together, renting an old shack by the beach. Mum managed a few walks and picnics, but I really noticed her slow, inevitable retreat from life. By the time we returned home she was sleeping more, and within a few weeks she was no longer taking her beloved daily beach walks with her dog Misty. She stopped reading books and watching videos, stopped answering the phone and writing emails soon after. Her world was becoming smaller by the day. We hung out with her, trying to keep cheerful, as well as sharing intimate moments crying and saying all that needed to be said.

Mum was now on an inner journey of her own. It was her wish not to prolong her life with more chemo or draining. With her particular cancer we were told that death usually comes from a bowel obstruction. Finally, with our support, Mum made the huge decision to stop eating. Three weeks later she had lost a lot of weight and was sleeping a great deal but still felt alive within herself. With her brother Clive also visiting from overseas, we managed a last picnic to her favourite beach.

As a family we got together with Zenith who gave us the professional support and advice we needed. She explained how events might unfold, and how it was possible to make all the arrangements for Mum's death ourselves. So when Mum died we didn't have to call a funeral director, Zenith could do the paperwork, and we could care for Mum's body, until we took her to the crematorium. We all agreed to this approach. It gave us confidence and peace of mind knowing how to deal with the final phase of Mum's passing.

Then Mum decided to stop drinking. Within a few days she became nauseous through dehydration. She had been sucking on ice cubes to moisten her mouth, then spitting out the water. She wanted to die. It was confronting for us. Her courage was inspiring. We did our best to support her in every way.

Her doctor visited and, with Mum in visible discomfort, was quite upset we had chosen this path without medical help. With medications given for nausea and insomnia, Mum was told that a few sips of fluid when thirsty would not prolong her life. We all felt emotional and confused. Before we knew it we were agreeing to morphine. Even with a mild dose, she quite rapidly lost her ability to speak and seemed confused. The inevitable, now rapid decline of this final stage hit me hard, even though I had known for a long time before that my mother's death was approaching. Although the morphine gave relief from the pain and let her sleep, her inability to speak concerned me, because there were times when she clearly wanted to communicate. Thankfully, there were also a few times when, with much-focused effort, she made herself understood.

Three days after Mum started the morphine, there was a concert for her in our living room. By now Zenith and Mum had formed a deep connection. Zenith organised her friends, Mum's favourite international musicians, Deva Premal and Miten, to come and play for her on Good Friday. Although I was apprehensive about this, Mum gathered enough energy to open her eyes and clearly let us know the concert must go on. So we created a beautiful space with cushions, rugs and mattresses, and on a small table in the centre of the room we made an altar, with flowers, candles, photos and Mum's most precious things on it. When the musicians arrived we carefully walked Mum into the sitting room where we lay her on a couch and wrapped her in a blanket.

She managed to communicate her gratitude to them and looked so happy and excited. The sacred music was blissful, giving each of us the opportunity to find celebration in the experience and allow the heaviness of the last few days to subside. When it was over and just close family were left, Mum pointed to, and half-reached out for, the floor beside the altar. We didn't know what she was doing. She was so frail, we rushed to assist her, bringing her a mattress to lie on. She was laughing at her own clumsy attempt and so were we. She wanted to lie on the floor beside the altar.

The afternoon drifted peacefully by. We lay in the beautiful golden light that filled the room, and were all held by the morning's music and Mum's peace. She drifted in and out of sleep, Misty at her side. By the evening her breathing was slow. After we rugged Mum up, we prepared dinner and opened a good bottle of wine, then sat at the dining table with Mum asleep behind us. It was the first time we had moved away from her the whole day. As we told stories and enjoyed our dessert, we suddenly noticed her breathing had changed. As we moved to be at her side it was clear these were her last breaths.

Zenith told us it was Mum's wish not to be touched in those last moments, as holding her may make letting go more difficult. This was a very confronting experience, as it appeared her body was gently gasping for air. I was right beside her, and closing my eyes I prayed for her peace and imagined her entering the path of light in the sky.

A few minutes later there was silence. She had left. It was beautiful and incredibly sad. Each of us was dealing with the emotion of the moment in our own way, our eyes closed, thinking loving thoughts and wishing her spirit well on its journey. I was in shock, grief and relief. Her beloved dog Misty got up and walked downstairs with her head low, she obviously knew what had happened. Over the next few hours, as we sat there with Mum's body, we spoke a little and quietly rearranged the objects from the altar onto the blanket covering her. She lay adorned with flowers, shells and photos, surrounded by flickering candles, her body honoured with our love and her memories.

The next morning, we called Zenith, who came to be with Mum. She brought out the letters Mum had written for us and placed them over Mum's heart, which was still warm. She completed the paperwork and comforted us. We called a few of Mum's close friends to come and be with her body. Later that afternoon we washed and dressed her, and placed her in the simple pine-and-rope coffin we had organised beforehand.

We had arranged for the crematorium to open the following morning on Easter Sunday. We took her there ourselves; only the immediate family was present. We planned to hold a special garden service for friends and extended family later. There were lots of flowers, photos and poems. We also had our letters from Mum, which we took turns to read in silence. In them, she told us of her love, her thanks and her surrender to the journey. She asked us not to grieve for too long, knowing that in spirit she is still with us.

It was such a deep journey, which left our lives changed forever. A time for letting go completely while always holding her in our hearts: a profound shared experience. Now as I re-live moments during those last months of her life, I recall when Mum and I lay together on her bed, holding hands and staring with love into each other's teary eyes. It was Mum's dying that helped me to open to true love without fear. Even in the sadness, I felt trust, peace and love in her heart. Only now do I realise that in those last few sharings, her tears were for me and my sadness. She was already free.

Thanks for showing me the way Mum. I love you.

David Hauserman

Getting the funeral organised

Arranging the funeral is usually the first thing you have to deal with after a loved one has passed away. You may simply want to use a funeral director to take care of everything for you. However, it is possible and legal to take care of all the details yourself, which can be more empowering and satisfying, or you may choose a combination of both.

If possible it helps to make enquiries ahead of time, as this takes the pressure off you in the final intense days or weeks of a loved one's life.

Funeral directors are there to help you, but they are also operating a business. Some are better than others and recommendations from friends can be useful. When you are talking with the funeral director, make notes of everything that is discussed. Don't be afraid to ask questions, and find out the costs. The time between death and the funeral is inevitably busy, but it can also be the start of accepting your loved one is gone and relinquishing your attachment to their physical presence.

Unless you are Jewish or Muslim, funerals do not need to take place immediately or even within a few days. It is totally acceptable to keep the body in a coolroom for up to several weeks. This allows for any family to arrive from around the country or overseas. Do not feel pressured to do anything in a hurry—you are the client. Make sure you get what you want, not what others think you should have.

Legal paperwork needs to be completed and plans for the funeral made. Before working out what you want for the ceremony, decisions will need to be made about dressing the body and who may want to view your loved one; some families like to have a vigil to keep your loved one company prior to the funeral.

It is customary to prepare the body before it is placed in the coffin. Washing and shampooing are often all that's required and family can do this. Make-up is optional. Embalming is not usually necessary, although it may be required for long-distance transportation, or if there is a very long delay before the funeral. Choosing clothes and dressing the person's body can give you an unexpected and satisfying sense of completion.

It is fine to leave jewellery on for the funeral although you should consider carefully whether or not you would ultimately like to keep treasured pieces for sentimental reasons or as family heirlooms. They could then be removed before the actual burial or cremation.

Putting various personal items into the coffin is discussed at length in 'Putting together the ceremony'.

The body, although often transported in a hearse, can be transported to the funeral in a range of vehicles, such as your car, a horse and cart, a much-loved Kombi, the farm truck, or customised motorbike and sidecar.

With the growing awareness of the health of the planet, people in many countries are opting for green funerals. Although you may be worried that a cardboard coffin might look cheap, there is no cause for concern. Green funerals can be expensive and lavish or simple and low budget. At a recent green funerals expo in London, the ultimate eco choices included felt shrouds decorated with leaves and also beautiful robes with seeds sewn into them that will germinate when buried.

Eco-friendly coffins, made from plantation timber, recycled cardboard, bamboo or simple pine with rope handles all break down easily. They can be left plain or transformed into something more personal. Whatever coffin you choose or, if you make one yourself, you can avoid the plastic liner by lining the coffin base with something absorbent such as a quilt, newspapers or sawdust.

Recycled cardboard coffins should be available through your funeral director. Some funeral directors are reluctant to use them or say they are not allowed—this is simply not true. If they don't stock them, ask them to order one for you from companies which produce them to official standard requirements. Some people worry that they may not be strong enough or may leak, but this is not the case. They are as strong as wooden coffins and are easily carried by pallbearers. The wonderful thing about eco-friendly coffins is they don't introduce toxins into the ground or, if burnt, into the atmosphere.

Different countries are utilising a range of local materials which allow for imaginative touches. In England they are using wicker, willow, and split bamboo. The possibilities for coffins are endless as discussed in 'Creativity in grief'. Choices range from eco-friendly coffins to building your own to the approved specifications. Small white coffins for children add a gentleness and covered baskets for babies are less confronting, as in the story of Indigo.

One lady who was afraid of the dark chose a split-bamboo coffin, as the woven bamboo let the light through. Clearly there are no right or wrong choices; it is a matter of what you feel is most appropriate.

Let the whole family be involved in the preparations.

THE INTIMACY OF DEATH AND DYING

Caring for my dying father at home

'While there is Death, there is Hope' were the words our dad Barry chose for his epitaph. His gentle acceptance of death was to deeply shape our lives.

A few years earlier Dad had no option but to put our mum, Roma, into a nursing home. He'd already given up work and dedicated many years of loving care to her, supporting Mum through a progressive loss of sanity, until caring for her at home was no longer possible. Finding himself alone in a big house, Dad sold the family home and came to live with me and my five-year-old daughter Georgia Rose. This restored a sense of family, since my marriage had recently ended. We took care of each other.

With a quick mind, wicked sense of humour and terrific zest for life, Dad enjoyed returning to work again as a doctor. Appearing far younger and more vibrant than his 75 years, he also knew he was living with a progressive lung disease. He wasn't afraid to speak about death, especially his own. Having encountered death many times he spoke about it with lightness and humour, imagining one day holding court from his deathbed surrounded by loved ones. So there was never any doubt in our minds he would die at home, although I had no idea of the challenges this would involve.

Dad had a number of years working before reluctantly admitting he was too breathless to walk the short distance from his car to the clinic. At this point, I assumed the role as his carer. I'd already nursed him through numerous bouts of sickness, including cancer, but Dad always got better. I laughingly told him he was a phoenix, rising immortal and invincible time and again.

When Dad became visibly unwell I confided in his doctor that I found it stressful adjusting to his increasing needs. When asking her for help, I was told to consider a nursing home, or to call an ambulance if seriously concerned. She didn't do home visits, failed to make suggestions about community or after-hours medical support I could access, and made no effort to provide information on how to care for Dad at home. She simply resigned from being his doctor. I rarely cry, but when I left the surgery I broke down. There was no way that Dad was going to end up in a nursing home! One parent in an institution was enough.

I had no idea how much information could be accessed easily through local palliative care services. I was lucky to find a wonderful new doctor specialising in palliative care and home visits. A friend running a nursing service provided a registered nurse for his personal care, and it turned out World War II veterans could access many services free or at minimal cost.

Dad expressed concern that the final stages of his lung disease could become unmanageable at home and that at the end of his life he might need to go to hospital. After years of being a doctor, becoming a patient made him no less vulnerable than anyone else. Fortunately the doctor and nurse assured him it was possible for him to die comfortably at home.

Georgia was only ten when her grandfather died. Some might have felt concern for a child living in a home where someone was dying, but I believe she learnt more about life by taking an active role in caring for him than any amount of formal education. She became a part of the caring team, and learnt that dying is a natural part of life and that with loving support it is possible to live fully until you die.

Was it easy? No, absolutely not. But many things in life which are truly worthwhile require effort to achieve. Had Georgia only been able to see her beloved grandfather during visiting hours in hospital it would have been far more difficult. At home she could share daily life with him, while gently coming to terms with the inevitability of his death. Later, when she faced the death of three grandparents within two years, she had an understanding and wisdom too few children have the opportunity to acquire.

I can honestly say I often felt quite overwhelmed by the enormity of my role as a primary carer. I didn't have much life outside home. Although family and in-home respite carers enabled me to continue to work, I was alone at night. I was always listening for the sound of my father's bedside bell—his signal for help—which meant playing music wasn't possible. I couldn't leave home unless someone was scheduled to take my place, which was often emotionally and logistically challenging.

While we had the support of many services, their primary focus was Dad. I secretly wondered if I could last the distance. Then I learnt about HOME Hospice. They provide volunteer mentors to support carers through the process of caring for a loved one dying at home. My mentor, Julie, was there for me. She focused on my needs as carer, giving me the strength to face the most demanding part of the journey. Naturally, friends and family were supportive too, but none of us had prior experience of what was required.

Julie's presence as a wise and knowledgeable friend enabled me to access the emotional and practical resources I needed to get through the final weeks. We organised a gathering of family and friends who were willing to be involved. I remember feeling the weight lift from my shoulders in a miraculous way.

The last phases were certainly the most challenging, yet there was something so precious and humbling about nursing a proud man who'd spent much of his life caring for others. To our surprise we were capable of far more than we dreamt possible. Depths of intimacy, honesty and expression emerged between us. Love was shown daily in words and gestures, and we all learnt the importance of leaving nothing unsaid.

In those last weeks Dad suggested we might want to send him to a nursing home. Always a considerate man, he needed to know that he wouldn't be a burden on his family. It added great richness to the remainder of his life for him to know how much we wanted to continue caring for him. He was determined to live until my sister Kate's wedding. He'd written his father-of-the-bride speech, and insisted I attend the wedding to read it, but for me to do this he had to go into a hospice for a few days. I found this extremely hard, as he was clearly so close to dying.

At 2 a.m. on the night before he was due home, the hospice called to say he was dying and to come quickly. Arriving, we found him unconscious, grey and rattling ominously. We refused to say goodbye. Instead we told him he would come home the next day to his precious cat and bedmate Danny Boy and reminded him all his family were not yet there. His eldest son was still a few hours away. I am absolutely certain what got Dad through that long night, against all odds, was his stoic determination to die at home in his own bed. A determination shared by his children.

One of my happiest moments was helping to lift Dad from the ambulance stretcher into his own bed again. Friends and family all let out a mighty cheer and joy abounded to see him where he belonged with Danny Boy purring contentedly in his arms.

The next day was time to fulfil another last wish, to see his beloved wife, Roma, for the last time. Getting Mum out of the nursing home wasn't easy. Her body was very twisted. As we wheeled her to his bedside he reached out, took her hand

and told her she was the love of his life. He said he had never forgotten his promise to love her in sickness and in health. This was a truly precious moment, vital to his desire to feel complete with his life.

Aware this was the last time my siblings and I would be together with our parents, it was a life-defining occasion, filled with laughter and tears. Dad shone with such brightness and vitality, his eyes sparkling, his skin so luminescent that he looked like he would live forever.

However, by the evening he began to experience difficulties. We were proud of our ability to look after him ourselves but wondered if we might need to call on 24-hour nursing care. Fortunately we didn't. We were able to administer all the drugs he required through a line placed under his skin. Having been told to ring the palliative care team with any questions at any time, I rang to check if Dad could have a stiff scotch with his morphine. Let me assure you, a dying man can have anything he wants!

On Dad's final day he was able to enjoy a hearty breakfast in his own bed, read his favourite newspaper, talk with his family and enjoy a short black coffee in his special demi-tasse cup. He was very frail, but was deeply contented and at peace with his life ending. By lunchtime his breath was laboured and he entered his dying process. We still included him in our conversations while we all sat around his bed sharing stories of his life and his elderly sister brought a tray of sandwiches.

Dad knew my brother's family was arriving that evening. Somehow we sensed he wouldn't die before they arrived. With tears in his eyes, Dad's cousin, a priest, administered the last rites and anointed him. The radio station Dad loved continued to play, announcing the passing hours, although for us time stood still.

When the last family members arrived, we opened a bottle of the finest champagne, charged our glasses and gathered around Dad's bed to toast him: 'To a life well loved and well lived.' Tenderly wetting his lips with champagne he joined us in a final toast to his life. What a moment of triumph! Our father was dying exactly as he had hoped—in his own home, surrounded by family, friends and all he cherished. I was so grateful to be able to tell him everything was just as he wanted and there was nothing to hang on for and, with those words, he took his final breath, Danny Boy still purring in his arms.

As he was at home, we didn't need to let Dad's body go until we were ready. Being able to take as much time as we needed gave us enormous comfort. Continuing to talk to him, expressing our appreciation and love for the inspirational man he'd been, we lit candles honouring the man we all loved. My brother slept beside his bed that night, keeping Dad company in death just as we had in life.

Danny Boy remained purring in Dad's arms for twenty hours after his death, leaving only briefly to eat. When the undertakers came, he reluctantly relinquished his post and sat beside the bed observing proceedings. Dad's body was taken, and Danny Boy walked down the path beside him then sat on the gatepost until the hearse disappeared.

Kate Maguire

A beloved pet can offer love and comfort.

Dying at home

Naturally, many people would rather die at home in their own bed, surrounded by family, friends and familiar things. In this way they can do as they please, in their own rhythm, unrestricted by hospital procedures and visiting times. Daily life can continue on around them. They are free to potter around their house or garden, and friends can visit in a relaxed way.

Until recently it was entirely normal to die at home, cared for by your family. Now, however, with time constraints, scattered families and eroded communities, there has come a greater need for palliative and hospice care.

The idea of looking after someone at home can be overwhelming so we tend to feel they might be better off in hospital because we feel unqualified for such a huge responsibility. These fears are very understandable.

If, however, you do decide to undertake home care for someone who is dying, it's important to fully understand their diagnosis and take into account certain practicalities to know if this is possible. The management of pain and medication can be daunting, but palliative care support systems (see 'Helpful websites and contacts') are so well organised these days that in most cases pain management can be dealt with within a home environment.

Doctors, community nurses and hospice and palliative care staff are all there to help you. Volunteers, local community organisations or church groups may also provide support. Some hospice services offer mentors to help families by talking through issues and giving practical advice, either in person, online or by phone. Others offer a team of volunteers to support the primary carer with the hands-on caring. That said, you mustn't feel a failure if, for some reason, your loved one needs to be moved to a palliative care unit or hospice for end-of-life care, as everyone's journey is different.

It helps to find a key contact for services in your area. For instance, your council or local government may have an aged-care officer. Many of the same requirements are needed by young and old when dying, so this is a good place to see what back-up is available to you. Pick up the phone or get on the internet or, better still, ask someone else to do this to support you. Friends love to have something practical and useful to do at these times.

Palliative care support for the dying, local hospitals and nursing systems will help you access practical resources such as the loan of wheelchairs, commode and shower chairs, bedpans and hospital beds. They can advise you where to buy items such as incontinence pads, bedliners and bedsore protectors to line the bed with, as these cannot be re-used for health reasons.

Keep a notebook for all the information you gather. You will find this an invaluable point of reference for everyone involved. This is a good time to talk about the importance of getting together a back-up team. It is challenging to support someone to die at home and it is not something to undertake alone. At some point the job becomes 24 hours a day, seven days a week, and everyone needs time for the basics of life such as sleeping, eating and bathing. It is often a great gift discovering how many people want to help and feel honoured to be asked. Family, friends, neighbours, work colleagues, children and even friends of friends can be included on the roster.

If you are highly independent and used to doing things on your own, it's a great time to be flexible. Collecting together a willing support team will change the whole experience for you, helping to ensure you don't become exhausted. You don't need to know exactly how people can help, just ask them what kind of availability they have and what support they can offer. People will suggest ideas that you may not have thought of and you will be surprised at the creativity and insights. Write down their contact details and what they have suggested, as you may be grateful for them later on.

A diary or a log book, kept in a central place in your home, such as by the phone or on the kitchen table, is the best means of communication for everyone as they come and go at different times. It holds all the information on the medications and pain relief required. It will include when and what to administer, what needs to be bought, done or given, and who needs to be informed and what has taken place. A diary or log book relieves the pressure of being the only one who knows what has to happen next. Many people also like to keep a journal where carers and visitors can enter their thoughts and feelings.

A person's mobility, size and bodily requirements also have to be considered. One family spoke of their sadness when their mother, who had broken her hip and was incontinent, had to be moved to a nursing home. They sadly had to concede that she needed to be somewhere with a mobile hoist. Their father, however, died at home, with a large team of supporters. Although he was unable to move himself, at the end he was very thin and light enough for a couple of people to manoeuvre him to keep him clean and pain free. While a family might have exactly the same intention and support systems, in some situations they may be unable to help someone die at home because of issues outside their control.

Most of us learn on the job, so make sure you ask questions and request help where needed. In spite of past incidents or family baggage, generally people will let go of any issues, to become real and supportive in the presence of the dying. Those who have cared for a loved one at home usually feel it is one of the most bonding and rewarding experiences of their lives. It can be a time 'out of time', when words become unnecessary and someone's calm, peaceful presence is what is ultimately required. So if this is the direction you'd like to take, the good news is that it may be entirely possible.

Losing my mother to Alzheimer's

I'd been hoping she would die for years. Sometimes I would just pray for God's mercy so my mum, Roma, would go peacefully. I had especially wished for this before we had to put her in the nursing home. It was not to be.

My mother had severe Alzheimer's and it was traumatic for everyone when we moved her from the home she'd lived in for years but no longer knew.

She was in a nursing home for six years. In that time she lost the power of speech and, after a broken hip, she forgot how to walk. In recent times she was being fed on mushy food, as even the simple act of chewing was beyond her. She wouldn't have wanted to live like that as she had been a woman of great beauty and grace. The loss of dignity would have horrified her.

My father always said, 'You girls aren't bad looking, but your mother, now she was a real beauty!' I suppose we could have been slighted at the comment, instead we enjoyed it, knowing she was 'the love of his life'. It was that great love that drove my father to keep looking after my mother at home for as long as he possibly could and far longer than he could manage.

When you lose someone to Alzheimer's, you lose them gradually, piece by piece, memory by memory. It's not a kind disease.
Mum just started drifting away, repetitive, slightly erratic. She
was still bubbly and enjoyed her children, though bit by bit she
needed help to do everyday things. She went through a very
childlike and loving stage, when she was very affectionate and
expressive. It is that time I will always remember most fondly
in my relationship with my wonderful mother.

Mum had always been a spirited, active woman, engrossed
in her children's lives, and enjoyed talking long into the night.
She loved celebrating each and every event with family, preparing delicious meals, and creating a warm and wonderful home.
Yet in the final year before my father almost collapsed from
caring for her, all she wanted to do was go home. Home
to her childhood home in Adelaide. Home to her father
who had died decades before. All her treasured belongings that
she had bought around the world were unknown to her. She
began spending long days in bed. Bathing was traumatic. It
involved stripping naked with her and showering together. At
some point she would realise she was naked with a stranger, as
I was to her then. A struggle would ensue to try and clean her
before conceding defeat.

In the midst of these terrible moments my dear sister Kate
and I would collapse in fits of not tears but laughter. It was
heartbreaking but somehow we could find the funny side of
being naked, trying to manage much-needed bathing, with our
mother crying 'HELP!'

By the time my father realised it was impossible to give her
the care she needed at home we were all exhausted. The nurses
were amazed we had continued so long. But to my father, left
alone in the family home, it just wasn't long enough.

It was hard to hand over the care of our mother and particularly hard, when visiting, to turn around and leave her. In the
early days she would try to follow which almost broke our
hearts. It's the hardest walk you will ever make. In later years I

would think of those times and almost wish there was still some response from her when I left.

Despite all this she would still greet my father with a sunny smile when he visited, as he did faithfully every day when he could still manage it. Being a retired doctor Dad enjoyed a jovial relationship with the nursing staff, grateful for the care they took of his beloved Roma.

My father had numerous health problems and had moved in with my sister, where he was cared for with great love until he died after a long and debilitating illness. Towards the end we would take Dad in his wheelchair with his oxygen bottle to visit my mother, where he would feed her chocolates and murmur to her while she gazed off with vacant eyes. He would often recite his favourite poem to her, and hold her hand with tears in his eyes.

On my father's last perfect day of life we brought my mother from the nursing home to spend the afternoon with him in his room. The next evening he died peacefully with his family around him, glad to have seen her one last time. We always thought the two of them were hanging around in this world for each other. My father couldn't bear to leave her, and perhaps in some corner of her remaining mind she didn't want to leave without him.

Nearly four months after our father's death, I received the call I'd been waiting for. My mother had suffered a stroke and was in a coma. They wanted us to come. It was the same day that Kate's child Georgia was being baptised at home. Georgia had helped look after her grandfather for many years, and had been around during the emotionally difficult yet wonderful times that were involved in caring for someone dying at home. As this was her special day, after months of grieving, my husband and I decided to go to be with Mum, leaving them to celebrate.

Though I had become used to my mother's deterioration, it was still a shock to find her so still and silent, curled around a pillow put in the bed to support her stroke-ridden side.

We spent many hours together. I talked about my life and marriage. She had never met my husband, and sadly he never knew the woman my mother used to be. I knew how much she would have loved him. I told her that after many years of searching for the right man, she could be at peace knowing I had finally found the person I wanted to spend the rest of my life with.

There's a sense of hopelessness at a time like this. When someone is in a coma it's a time of waiting, so we were left to contemplate our thoughts and memories, to talk to her and hold her hand, and make sure she knew she was loved. I told her that all her children were happy and that she didn't need to worry about any of us. I wanted her to know there was nothing to hang on for, and that Dad was waiting for her.

Kate and Georgia visited with the priest, Brian, who had administered the last rites to my father with tears in his eyes. He now conducted the same blessing for my mother, and I am sure that was what she wanted. My brother Tony arrived after the baptism and eventually, after many hours, we left him there to sleep beside my mother's bed.

All that night I slept lightly, expecting the call that finally came in the early hours of the morning. Tony thought the end was near. So we went back to my mother. My eldest brother Tim arrived mid-morning.

We all officially entered the twilight zone. Mum had been sharing a room, but the nursing home found another place for her roommate, so the four of us moved in. Of course we expected her to go at any time, but she had her own plans. We thought she was enjoying having us all around her too much to go anywhere! Although we'd often visited in groups there had never been a time when all four children had visited together. We already had many photos in her room but we brought more in, and at night we lit candles and rubbed cream into Mum's hands.

Have you ever lived in a nursing home? Well, we did. For four days and three nights we were at the nursing home together, sleeping in her room on cobbled-together chairs or water chairs. The nursing home provided tea and biscuits, and we only left to get food to bring back.

It was a strange sleep-deprived time, waking, if we'd slept, with each four-hourly visit by the nurses to check Mum's condition or to administer more morphine. After a while we lost all sense of day and night. All that mattered was being together and honouring our mother with our memories, stories, laughter and tears. My family has always managed through difficult times with a humour sometimes perceived by others to be quite black, but it was a choice of laugh or cry.

At times the nurses would ask us to leave the room so they could change our mother's clothes and sheets. We hovered uncertainly outside the door, not sure how far to go, longing to stay close in case they thought she was slipping away.

Mum's room was at the end of the corridor, and in the middle of the night the nursing home was still and quiet. The wheelchairs were left in a corner for the new day. One night, tired as I was, I pulled one out, sat in it, then wheeled around a bit. My siblings each grabbed a chair and we had impromptu wheelchair races up and down the corridor. It was a moment of hilarity and bonding I will always remember. There can actually be moments of silliness and laughter in the midst of pain and sorrow.

It was touching to discover just how much people in the nursing home cared for our mother. Staff members came to sit with her and share their memories of her. They talked of her smile and sweet nature, and gently said their goodbyes to a woman they had looked after so intimately. To see them take time at the end of their shift, or the beginning of their day, to visit her and spend time with us was so touching, humbling and inspiring. It wasn't just a nursing home, it had become our mother's last and final home. That meant so much.

I will never forget one nun who spent time with Mum and said in her Irish brogue, 'God's ready for you, my darlin'. You don't need to wait, he's got a place ready for you now, and it's alright to leave.' We kept repeating that message, 'It's okay to go. We're all here together now. Dad is waiting for you, he's there holding out a hand to you. All you need to do is take his hand.'

Towards the end, one of the nurses came to bathe our mother. Kate and I helped to undress Mum and massage cream into her skin. It had been years since we'd seen our mother naked, when trying to get her to shower with us. Her pale skin was soft and smooth and her near-bare pubic region was a testament to her age, sexuality and mothering. This was the woman who had given birth to and nursed all of us. I am so grateful to have had the chance to intimately care for my mother in the way she cared for me. Those moments around my mother's bed, with my sister and the nurse, are some of the most memorable moments of our time together before her death.

I wasn't there when she took her last breath. Every time I left the room for a toilet or food break or to walk down the corridor to get some air, I said goodbye and told her she was free to go. Sometimes I said it silently, sometimes in words or tears, but I said it every time. I was there when my father drew his last ragged breath, but I wasn't there when my mother finally started on the journey to rejoin her soulmate.

I have no regrets about that. We'd spent so many precious hours together, and I had said everything I would ever want to say to her. We were both at peace. My siblings were with her in a room full of family photos, and had great love for the mother who had loved us so well. I miss her still and will never forget that time spent with my sister and brothers while Mum finally left her tired mind and body behind, to be young, beautiful and free once again.

Roma died just a few days short of four months after her husband Barry. Their ashes are scattered around and up inside a Morton Bay fig in a city park. It is our *family tree*. We visit there on anniversaries and birthdays, and when we want to spend some time remembering all the years of love they shared with us. After their beloved cat died on Mum's birthday we scattered his ashes there also. We miss them, we'll always miss them, but they both died with their family around them, words of love echoing in their ears, and that's all any of us can hope for.

Anna Maguire

Dying in hospital or a hospice

The difference between a hospice and a hospital is that a hospice is a palliative care facility specifically for the dying, where they are not trying to keep patients alive but simply as comfortable and pain free as possible, in an atmosphere of quiet acceptance by both patients and staff.

If your loved one wants to die in hospital, or if a hospital is the best option for a peaceful end, one of the most important things you can help with is maintaining their dignity since hospital patients don't have the same control as at home over what happens to them. When they eat, sleep, shower and receive visitors revolves around hospital schedules. This can be challenging for independent people.

Hospital staff are busy and this is sometimes frustrating. It helps when patients or their families ask questions about what is happening, about treatment options and so on.

If possible it is important for families to know the wishes of their loved one prior to hospitalisation as they may have to make decisions on their behalf. Do they want 'active treatment' or just to be kept comfortable? Often, elderly patients say they feel they have lived a good life and don't want to be around any longer but, unless it is documented, medical staff are required to keep them alive. If a person doesn't have a NFR (not for resuscitation) order in place, medical staff are obliged to treat them, even if they believe it is not in their best interest. If a patient 'crashes'—for example, has a heart attack—medical staff must attempt to resuscitate them, even if they are elderly with brittle bones. Resuscitating an older person who is fragile can be tough, as it can break ribs. If you don't know what questions need to be asked, it's a good idea to talk to staff about what you need to know and what decisions may lie ahead.

Caring for the dying is a very special calling. It's inspiring to realise the depth of connection nurses have with dying patients, considering they are dealing with death so often. Being in the presence of one death is life changing; we can only guess what it must mean to be a nurse. To do what they do with such love, nurses need to set aside connections they have made with their patients over the years and concentrate on delivering compassionate, professional care in the moment, as Fiona, a nurse experienced in working with those who are dying, explains: 'Even nurses who seem stern will focus on meeting the patient's needs in the time of dying. It touches everyone's heart. Death is often undignified; that is just the way it is. Bowels and bladders which no longer have control can be confronting. Nurses work to make sure such issues are dealt with in as dignified a fashion as possible, for patients and family alike. Nurses are particularly capable of meeting patients' needs because they know what to expect. They know how to keep their patients safe, pain free and treated in a way that doesn't add to the difficulty of losing control and independence.'

There can be issues for family and friends in dealing with their loved ones in their final days or weeks. Fiona believes that people who don't want to be a burden are generally more likely to want to die in hospital. 'They often push their family away and become abrupt,' she says. 'It is their way of holding onto their dignity. This is sad for the family, who can find it hard to understand, as they frequently want to love and support their relative until the end. For a person to feel they have lost face by getting sick and no longer having control over their body, having their loved ones seeing them die can feel very undignified. Most of us don't want pity, and find it embarrassing.'

Fiona says that even after someone has died, nurses still treat them as they would wish to be treated. 'When I am cleaning up their body getting it ready for their family, I still talk to them as if they were alive. "Buddy I'm just getting you ready, all your suffering is over now and you are going to a better place."' It can be common practice for nurses to open the window to release the spirit and lay flowers on the person's chest before the family come to view them.

'When we ring, to tell relations their loved one has died, we feel it is important to give them time to take it in,' Fiona explains, 'so we often suggest they take their time, ring relatives and friends, and we will ring them back in a while to organise the details. After a patient dies most facilities are as accommodating as possible even if the bed is needed for another patient. We never move someone out if the family hasn't seen them, even if it requires moving them to another part of the hospital. If we are really short of beds, sometimes they are taken to the mortuary, but we avoid that if at all possible.'

It can be difficult for nurses to talk to a family about their plans straight after someone has died, so it is helpful to have booked a funeral home beforehand to avoid the difficult task of finding one at short notice.

Religious requirements are very important in our multi-cultural world, and it's good to know hospitals are obliged to take into consideration all religious beliefs. Nurses are required to follow religious guidelines to the letter. If, for instance, one is not allowed to touch the body, they will always honour these needs. Hospital staff will do their utmost to ensure that a patient's dignity remains intact right to the end.

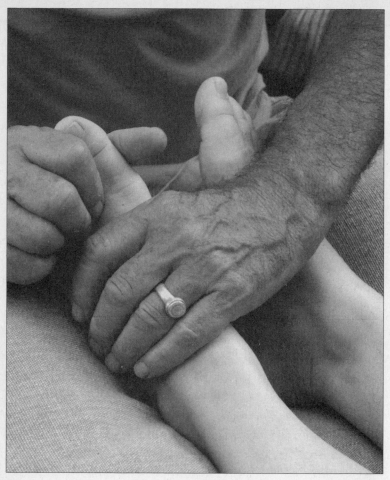

A gentle massage can soothe the body and mind.

The magic of a dying wish

Trish and I met as single mothers with toddlers. It was to become a friendship that lasted the next 28 years. She was certain her brother Alex and I were meant to be lovers and so brought us together. Our children will forever belong to the same family. We were always there for each other, no matter what.

Trish had recently lost a lot of weight after going on a liver-cleansing diet. She looked beautiful and was so proud of herself. Work was going well. She was healthy and had a loving, stable relationship with her partner Greg. They were planning to get married the following year, on the anniversary of their first date, six years earlier. Her son Kristian, sharing a house with them and Greg's son Luke, was also in a great relationship. Life had never been so good. She was at a point where she felt worthy enough to start looking for her daughter, her first child, who had been adopted out with much pain when Trish was sixteen.

After many ups and downs it was so wonderful to see Trish find her own much-deserved happiness and peace—until she announced she had inoperable cancer. All those who loved Trish kept asking how life could choose this moment to deliver such a cruel blow.

Those first few months we were all in denial. Trish organised barbecues, parties and all manner of social gatherings, drawing around her those who had fallen away over time. Old friends came to visit and stay. At first she thought she had energy enough for it all, but before long she realised she was exhausted.

Greg and Trish's old sandstone home was damp and difficult to heat in winter, and access was up a steep driveway. It soon became clear Trish needed to be on a single level, in a compact dry home with such facilities as a shower with room for a chair. Trish's cancer was now impacting on the extended family, threatening to split them apart. Trish could no longer look after them or herself—she needed the input and energy of a much larger group.

Greg found a new apartment to rent, set back from the road, close to the sea. Family and friends helped them pack up and dispose of many of their things. As well as dealing with Trish's illness, they were now dealing with the huge stress of moving house.

Although her new home was beautiful there was a veil of sadness around Trish as she stepped into it. Once a fiercely independent, private person Trish now found herself in the hands of her many friends and carers. She could only look on. Her wild, spontaneous life had been shaved back to a neat one-bedroom apartment overlooking a little walled, tiled patio. It is important for us to appreciate how those who are dying can feel so out of control as their independence is stripped away.

Trish was travelling at high speed through stages of life we usually expect to have lots of time for. Many possessions she had collected throughout her well-lived life were now gone. She wasn't even able to be there for her beloved son Kristian, who now had to find somewhere else to live. Practicalities were taking over. Space was needed for the wheelchair and other medical equipment. It was the beginning of winter and a very low time for everyone.

Once they had moved into the apartment it was agreed a team of three would be her constant carers. Trish, like so many people, didn't want those she didn't know intimately handling her. She asked if just Greg, her friend Rhonda and I would do this for her. We organised time slots that worked in and around our own schedules. Rhonda, a single mum, couldn't do early mornings but could manage days. I was working full-time and could do nights. Greg took over from me in the early hours of the morning until Rhonda arrived. Greg would go to work whenever he could. He was lucky to be blessed with a boss of great compassion who was happy to support him in any way he could.

My partner Alex took over our family responsibilities, freeing me up as needed. Somehow, despite juggling a team of eight at work, I was still able to be with Trish for those vital moments. They say it takes a village to truly grow a child; I believe it also takes a village to truly support a person's dying. There are many whose kind unexpected actions created treasured experiences. The women I worked with became my loving support team. When Trish was rushed to hospital, violently ill at 2 a.m., needing another kidney stent operation (she must have had six of these), the support was there for me to be with Trish and Greg.

The miracle was that Trish always awoke after these assaults on her body with a cheeky smile on her face. Even though her body was so frail, she'd crack outrageous jokes as if she could go on forever.

It was a rollercoaster ride. That same afternoon as Trish came out of her latest kidney stent operation I held the devastated Greg in my arms. He finally began to cry, berating himself for getting impatient with her demands. 'She's dying for God's sake, she's dying. How could I?'

We were all at breaking point. Until this moment no-one had admitted what we all knew. We were crumbling inside, knowing we were losing her.

In the midst of all the much-needed medical support, we managed to get the paperwork required for Greg and Trish to marry at a moment's notice. While organising this, Greg realised he had never divorced his son's mother who had left them seventeen years before. Somehow, Greg organised the divorce. All the wedding papers were signed and put away. Trish was still holding onto her dream of an October wedding. She had chosen a wedding dress pattern, but hadn't been strong enough to get out to choose the material.

By this time we had been directed to a carer's support program through the local council. Once a week, as a team, we had a two-hour break to release the mountains of emotions we were storing, by talking with our counsellor Richard. He allowed us to cry, rage, laugh, give up and give thanks for the blessings we were receiving. Being so close to death reminded us to hold sacred every breath we ourselves took. His unconditional acceptance was one of the most important gifts given to us. Carers are often so focused on those they are caring for that they lose sight of the energy draining out of themselves and forget to replenish it.

When it became too difficult for Trish to get in and out of her waterbed, palliative care organised a hospital bed for her. We placed it at the glass doors of the patio so she could look out. We knew she was running out of time.

Our world had shrunk to one room and one intention: to make Trish as comfortable as possible. Everything focused on pain relief. The cancer had spread from her cervix to her lymph glands, kidneys and liver. She was in extreme pain. All other concerns were put aside as we concentrated on keeping her comfortable. Anne, our palliative care nurse, often came in the early hours of the morning, as this seemed to be when Trish had the most difficulty. We became highly proficient in palliative care and pain management through 'on the job' training. It's remarkable what people are capable of when there's no other option. We learnt what drugs were needed for what outcome, how to administer them and how to recognise early the signs that more medication is required.

One Friday morning late in August after a particularly miserable night, something clicked inside me. I knew we were near the end. I called Trish's father, Bennie, who lived a flight away and had no idea Trish was so ill and dying; he had a cataract operation booked the following week and wondered if he could come up after that. I explained the urgency. Greg would tell Trish he wanted to marry her immediately, while Bennie was there. He promised to come right away.

The rest of the day was taken up collecting together family and friends to organise a magical wedding, if Trish agreed to bring it forward.

Bennie arrived late at night, exhausted and shaken at the sight of his only daughter. Putting his fear to one side, he joined Greg in his excitement about the wedding plans. Now there was no reason to delay. Greg was determined to marry Trish the next day. Of course she said yes, before drifting back into a fitful sleep. From that moment Bennie kept a vigil by her side. Refusing a bed, he slept upright on the sofa next to her for the next three nights.

We had eight hours to create a wedding. Miracles do happen.

In spite of her busy schedule, having previously committed to being available at a moment's notice, Julie, the marriage celebrant, agreed to come at five. Regardless of Trish's imminent death we were only able to proceed because the legal paperwork had previously been completed and signed more than the required month in advance.

Beautiful flowers were collected from the markets; expensive champagne arrived with crystal glasses engraved with Trish and Greg's names. The jeweller from down the street turned up with rings. Those chosen were fitted to their fingers in an impossible timeframe. Such kindness from strangers.

The local markets provided a perfect, crushed velvet outfit sparkling with little crystals that Trish could comfortably wear. By this time the cancer had distended her stomach and her comfort was the most important consideration. Karina, a hairdresser friend of mine, spent hours gently applying Trish's make-up and adorning her hair with delicate flowers. Along with the personalised wedding cake, beautiful food was organised.

For a while I found myself alone with a sleeping Trish and exquisite decorations with which to adorn her sacred space. I realised then what an extraordinary journey Trish had taken me on. Sometimes during the night vigils I would feel so strongly that the pain was like that of giving birth, and I could no longer distinguish between the process of birthing or dying. The intensity of these two experiences is equally profound. Anne, our palliative care nurse, told me, 'I have seen this phenomenon often while working with people who are dying and can't help but be in awe of the blurred lines between life and death which somehow bring everything around full circle.' And now, here I was involved in the preparations for one of the most powerful moments in life—the commitment of love between two people to support each other through life until death parts them.

The unique experience left Julie, the marriage celebrant, in total awe. She recalls: 'Patricia's condition had deteriorated— she was close to death. I came as soon as possible after my previous wedding. All my years as a celebrant could not have prepared me for the staggering contrast of the two occasions. The first was a big society wedding with a cast of hundreds. When I entered this other world everything changed. Loving friends and family had worked some kind of miracle—it was so beautifully festive, with all the attentions to detail traditionally the result of months of fuss and planning. In the centre of it all lay Trish, fragile and dying, but exquisitely dressed and very alert—she quickly pointed out a mistake in my hastily prepared certificate. At her side Greg, attentive to her every need, cherished each moment with the woman he loved so much. Their joy clearly transcended the unspoken dread of their parting.

'I felt so privileged to be conducting the ceremony. I was painfully aware that I must avoid clichés, which would be meaningless that day. Everyone is supposed to cry at weddings, yet we were all simply happy as the two lovers exchanged their vows with a quiet, secret intensity and depth of emotion that was precious beyond words.'

After the ceremony a euphoric Greg took Trish on a wheelchair sprint around their tiny patio. It was a blissful moment. When we gently put Trish back into bed she even drank a sip of champagne, having only been able to suck ice cubes for days previously. Trish's drug schedule had been carefully worked out the night before to make the best use of her precious life energy. She shone so brightly for the hour of her wedding then faded gently into another world. As she slept, the party gracefully continued around her into the night. To some it may seem strange to party in the presence of a dying person, but Trish wouldn't have had it any other way. Celebrating life was something she had excelled at.

Greg woke me in the early hours of the morning. He was too tired to even remember what drugs were needed to keep Trish's pain at bay and asked if I would take over. Angels sat with me that morning, I am certain. Little else was of importance other than overhearing the conversation Trish had before dawn with her mother who had died three years before. Memories arose for me then of once being told that the dying often talk to those who have gone before them, just as they themselves are leaving.

The next day, her body spent, Trish slept in a cocoon of drugs as her loving family and friends came and went. By now she had worn out every last breath.

As the first birds sang at dawn and with the rain gently blanketing us in a lacy mist, Trish left us. Surrounded by those she loved the exquisite bride chose the perfect moment to leave, reminding us of those lovely words 'My death is my wedding with eternity'.

The celebration did not end there. All day people crowded into the tiny apartment, some sitting on each other in order to fit, playing both sad and joyful songs on the guitars Trish had so loved. Telling stories, reading, singing and cracking naughty jokes, eating and celebrating her outrageous life. We kept her close to us all day. Being in the presence of Trish's body allowed us to see clearly that her essence no longer resided there. Her presence was palpable but no longer constrained within the small space her body had taken up. Late in the day the undertakers arrived to take her body.

Honouring her wish to be touched only by those she felt safe with, three of us, including her adored young niece, wrapped her body, still in her wedding dress, in sheets, put her into the body bag and lifted her gently onto the trolley.

Involving even the younger ones in her journey of death, right to the end, Trish had honoured her commitment 'to take us all with her on one heck of a ride'. She opened doors to previously unknown, yet extraordinary places. Even though Trish could not now put into practice in life the lessons we all learnt on this journey, her ripples will forever gently caress the edges of our lives. She continues to guide us ever onwards towards larger, more magnificent family experiences. Since Trish's death, her daughter Tash, adopted out 30 years before, has been brought to life for us all. Being in Tash's presence is uncannily like being with Trish again.

Trypheyna McShane

Supporting someone with a terminal illness

Sooner or later we will all die, but the difference for someone facing a terminal illness is that they have an approximate timeframe for their death. Naturally, this can be confronting for the person and those who love them, often leaving them overwhelmed and unable to see a way forward.

Although devastating, on reflection people often find that terminal illness has brought an honesty to their lives and in a strange way blessed them, by helping them reassess and discover what really mattered.

When Kathy, a hospice patient with terminal cancer, realised she only had a short time left, she decided to start an acknowledgement project, and left a beautiful legacy by encouraging us to take action now:

> Knowing, really knowing, your days on this earth are numbered is a true gift. I know you find it hard to believe but it truly is a blessing. We all live our lives as though there will always be a tomorrow to do the things we want to do and say. Knowing my days are numbered has given me the opportunity to receive love and acknowledgement,

and allowed me to live in the now in a way that was never available to me before. First, you could write to someone and acknowledge them for the contribution they have made to the world. Second, you could write and acknowledge them for the contribution they have made to your life personally. Finally, you could clean up a bad feeling or resolve an issue that has been plaguing a relationship. So many times we let our relationships go bad or ignore problems because there will always be tomorrow to fix it. Don't wait. Do it today. Let the ripple become a wave. If each of you participates in this project, think of how we will contribute to our lives, the lives of friends and what we truly only have, the moment of now.

Those who work with the dying have observed that often our fear of death is in fact our fear of pain. Dying can have painful moments—physical pain and discomfort, the emotional pain of saying goodbye and wondering what will happen next. The good news is that there are many stepping-stones to help you along, so you may benefit from the gifts this time offers. It may not be possible to control what happens but you can control how you react and respond to it. Often, the people who are the most joyous are the ones who face their grief and pain.

As you become familiar with the situation a loved one is in, try to relax a little. This allows your intuition to develop so you can add loving touches to transform your experience and theirs. Simple things you do make all the difference in keeping them comfortable, physically and emotionally. Holding, touching or gently massaging them can be wonderfully nurturing, if they like being touched. Ask them what they like. People with weight loss feel the cold and may need the comfort of woolly hats and warm bedsocks. Gentle healing music can create an atmosphere of calm. Silence too can be golden.

Simply notice what needs to be done—you don't need permission or instructions—but be sensitive that change can be disturbing. Allow yourself to stay open to what each day brings. Not everything can be planned but you'll achieve so much more by responding with a compassionate heart rather than trying to control everything. This is a big time for you. Take time out to be quiet. Just sit and feel, and don't always be doing. Allow yourself to be guided by quiet intuition, so often ignored in our fast-paced life.

Greg, who lost his soulmate Trish, says of his journey: 'I can't believe there is anyone who will not feel they have become a better person after going through an experience like this. The only way not to grow from this is to have shut a part of yourself down. The most profound lesson I learnt now travels through my daily life: don't sweat the small stuff, in the end it all disappears and is forgotten.'

Having spent a long time with someone with a terminal illness, how will you know when death is near? You may notice there is generally an attitude change and lack of interest in food. There may be up to 20 per cent loss of body weight or considerably more. Or if they are on cortisone or other medication, this can cause massive weight gain. Dehydration is often constant towards the end. By this stage people are often very weak. Even sucking water from a straw may be too difficult. You may have to moisten the person's lips with a little sponge or ice cubes. Another sign is that they detach from the world and start to look inwards. Whereas once they may have been avid readers, loved to watch television or listened to the news, all of this will drop away. This helps them concentrate on their journey ahead, and can be a precious time as you see the essence of the person you love more clearly and that part of them you will always love.

During this time supporting a person's senses is important—beautiful smells, warmth and fresh air really help, especially when someone is confined in a room. Although their ability to eat and drink may be minimal, the smell of delicious food can still be a pleasure. Often, cups of tea are asked for that will never be drunk, but they hold a memory of times past when sharing tea together was treasured. Make the bed with new beautiful soft bedsheets. Surround them with beauty. Introducing plants is a lovely idea as they can give continuity to those left behind. It is valuable to know that hearing is the last sense to go, so talking to someone who seems unresponsive or in a coma is still important. They may also start to have visions of their loved ones who have already gone.

Try to be aware of the needs of the person. Some want family and friends gathered around them, while others prefer to be left alone. Some people want to be held and touched as they die, others don't. Everyone's journey is different. Peace is very important during a person's last moments. This is an unparalleled time for spiritual work as there are no other distractions.

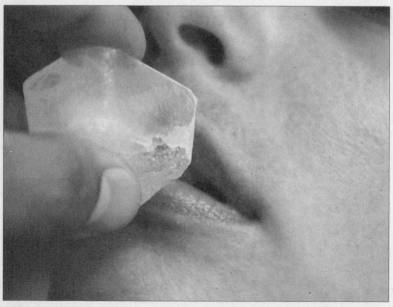

Bring an ice cube or moist sponge to someone's lips.

Single, but not alone

I cannot remember when I first learnt that Marcus had AIDS. Initially it was not something that caused him to change his lifestyle. He worked as long as he could in his job as a carer for people with intellectual disabilities. I always loved working with Marcus; he was such fun. He thought nothing of calling in to the residential care house on the weekends to take one of the clients out to the beach with him or to town for a coffee.

Marcus had that rare gift of nonjudgement, allowing him to love almost everyone, and in return he was much loved by many. He always talked of his family with great affection. He was adopted and at one stage decided to trace his natural mother, then suddenly stopped, saying, 'I slid down the rainbow into the best family and besides, what am I to say, "Hello, I am your son and I have AIDS!"'

Marcus lived in a wooden bungalow in a beautiful rural valley that was regularly cut off during the rainy season. The house was decorated by his mother Val's beautiful paintings, of which he was extremely proud. Often on a Saturday night we would meet at his house and head off together to a dance in a local country hall. Marcus was a flamboyant and charming character, with long, luxurious dark curls, resplendent in his fabulous red-leather jacket. Somehow, the dancing nights came to an end, but still everyone would gather at his house to chat, drink tea and listen to music. It was hard to grasp what was happening to our vibrant friend.

Marcus never became lost in regret. Whenever he had the energy, he would be at his favourite coffee shop eating chocolate cake and holding forth. Gradually, these days became further apart. Marcus got thinner. His hair was now much more sparse and straight as the energy drained from his body.

I remember being astounded one day to find him at a local restaurant, catheters hidden under his clothing. Physically he was so weak that he needed a wheelchair, but he was heartily enjoying the company and his meal. Such was this young man's indomitable spirit. How we loved him.

Marcus would regularly call me to ask my advice on various symptoms he was experiencing. On one of those days I had an early morning call asking me how I was and how the children were doing. When I asked him in return how he was, he told me of an ominous dream he had the night before. In it a great bird had descended upon him, then he casually enquired if it was daylight yet. 'I'm fine but I seem to have gone blind.' He had been like this for hours, but hadn't wanted to bother anyone. This was so typical of Marcus: calm, altruistic and accepting what to anyone else would have been a frightening situation. He agreed it might be a good idea to seek medical advice.

He had special glasses made. Marcus even managed to enjoy these new circumstances, insisting on buying new sunglasses for me in the process! So here was Marcus with dark glasses and a walking cane to support his failing sight. I persuaded him to stay the night at my place for chicken soup and a warm fire. As he had become thinner, with no body fat to sustain his body temperature, he started to really feel the cold. It was increasingly difficult to keep him warm; layered clothing, a beanie and scarf were all a necessity even in our mild winters.

I remember, too, Marcus's struggle with meningitis and hospitalisation. I went to visit him one Sunday, an orchid plant in hand to cheer up his bleak, white-walled hospital room, but he would have nothing of it. He pleaded with me to take him home, telling me the air in the hospital was 'polluted' and the nursing staff were all fakes, and that he absolutely had to leave.

I remember speaking with close friends Pam and Peter, and jointly coming to the conclusion that he would be more peaceful and emotionally stable at home in his familiar surroundings. Fortunately there were a number of us who were registered nurses or had nursing experience which made this a possibility. I announced my decision to the nurses in his ward who, taken aback, tried to insist that Marcus stay and that a formal clearance be given by his doctor. Being a Sunday this was impossible, so I reiterated we were leaving and that his medications needed to be made up. I started to pack up his belongings and headed down to emergency to borrow a wheelchair. His tablets were delivered and I was handed the discharge papers to sign—quite a breakthrough! We all knew to die at home would be a much more comforting journey for Marcus and for us, his carers.

Then we began the long drive home. I became increasingly alarmed at Marcus's delirium. I stopped at one stage to buy him a drink. Somehow he left the car and started following me into the café. As I returned him to the car he got stuck, unable to walk any further, and needed to be lifted back into his seat. I remember thinking on that long drive back he might die.

When we reached his home I gratefully handed him over to his friends who were now all waiting for him. They had moved his bed into the sitting room to make nursing him easier. Unfortunately this rearrangement of his furnishings added to his distress and confusion. That night, as Maria cared for him, he went through the house making odd piles of his possessions for his friends, then he put on music and danced bewitchingly on the tables.

We arranged a 24-hour roster to ensure Marcus was always looked after, and his local doctor offered to oversee his medical care. In those days caring for a dying person at home was virtually unheard of. Most people still went to hospital when they became seriously ill or bedridden.

At that time, people with HIV/AIDS were the subject of much derision and discrimination. It was the dreadful days of the TV ads, designed to instil fear into the hearts of those with little knowledge of the disease. They were isolated, treated by staff wearing masks, gowns and gloves, and visiting families also had to take these precautions. Their food was passed in through a hatch. So many young men died alone as parents and friends turned away from them. It's hard to believe now, that this is how it was.

We promised Marcus he was not going to die alone in a hospital bed surrounded by fear. We were determined to care for him ourselves with his dignity intact. Being so loved, there were many willing hands to help.

That week, as his confusion continued, the decision was made to take him up to a Tibetan Buddhist centre with a hospice attached. Teachings and a healing ceremony were a part of their practice. We felt that this spiritual presence would help Marcus's confused state. Calming meditations and prayers were held especially for Marcus to help him in his dying process. Afterwards, in the days following Marcus's return from the hospice, we felt we had our Marcus back, free from delusions, happy and at peace. In the following months Buddhist monks became frequent visitors to Marcus's home and as a result the idea of a local hospice service arose.

In the closing days of Marcus's life his once youthful body became gaunt and tired, his walk became a shuffle. His compromised immune system made him susceptible to chest and urinary infections. His temperature would soar. We would wait anxiously for the antibiotics to kick in. His dresser became lined with pill bottles and medication charts. Oral morphine was started to help with his aching body and slowly increased in time with the relentless march of the AIDS virus. Maria moved into his house to ensure that he would never be alone between our rostered shifts. We all travelled the long and winding road to his door at our given times.

Local restaurants would send out food, the hospital sent medications and clean linen, even the elderly ladies at the post office would mail Marcus cards wishing him well. I remember someone coming and playing Marcus sweet harp music. His acupuncture and chiropractic friends arrived to treat his back pain and offer comfort. When the monks were in town, they would drop by and pray with Marcus. It just did not seem possible that a time would come when all this was no longer necessary.

Being a working single mother, I generally took two or three night shifts each week. I would come with tasty tid-bits to tempt his appetite and my uni books under my arm in case there was an opportunity to study for my exams. Marcus always managed to raise a smile. We would hold each other, drink tea and chat a little. Sometimes he would cry out in the night. I would hurry to his side to soothe him. He would smile and reassure me he was alright. He would grow hot and I would cool him down with a damp cloth, turn the fan up, change his sheets and encourage him to drink water.

There came a time when conversation started to weary him. He asked Maria to limit his visitors. His loving mother would fly in regularly. Sometimes his father, brother and sister were also able to come. We were all aware that the end was getting close but kept willing away the inevitable. His body was so very frail now, although his strong, young heart kept on beating.

Marcus made plans for his funeral, he chose the music, he wanted dancing, balloons and his coffin placed behind a velvet curtain on a pedestal in the park. He seemed to relish organising these details for his own farewell.

About a week before he died, Marcus was carried outside and put in the hammock to be bathed. On another occasion he travelled on a bed in the back of a van, so he could see his beloved beach one last time. It was so very hard watching someone you love slip away before your eyes and feel helpless to do anything but watch and pray. Above his bed was written the Buddhist mantra, *Om Mane Padme Hum*, the sacred mantra of compassion for transformation and purification. Marcus took to slipping a card bearing the Blue Medicine Buddha, who is the representation of healing, inside his shirt and I would whisper the mantra each time I entered his room. His home became a hallowed place, and Marcus remained ever gracious and accepting of his journey.

We came to the last week. Marcus was confined to bed, his family by his side. Many friends gathered with their children in the garden. The weather now was so hot; it hadn't rained for ages. The fan was constantly on. His doctor would call by each day but there was now little to do beyond keeping Marcus comfortable. To comfort him, we moistened his lips, massaged his feet and turned him every two hours; we also made countless cups of tea to sustain ourselves. A hoist was placed over the bed to help Marcus adjust himself but soon it took two people to move him and tend to his needs.

The day before Marcus died, I was called to his bedside and, leaving my children with my housemate, found he had suffered a major epileptic seizure. I quickly administered Valium to relax him, and lay him on his side. Later that morning, I had to leave as my young son needed me. I kissed Marcus on his forehead and as I turned to go, he whispered 'Thank you' and managed a half wave. If I close my eyes, I can still see this scene as if it were yesterday. I am forever grateful to have been able to say my last farewell and feel that we helped him to die well, peacefully, at home, cared for by loving friends.

On the last morning, I was again called to his bedside after yet another seizure. He told his mother he felt like a clock ticking down. His eyes had been open for the past 24 hours, searching, seemingly questioning. Gradually he relaxed. He was now semi-conscious. So with all his closest carers gathered we chanted *Om Mani Padme Hum* to help him on his way.

We stroked Marcus, refreshed his skin when it was clammy and held onto each other and his parents. Realising he could no longer swallow his morphine, I drove to town to see his doctor, hurried to the chemist with the prescription, and returned to find Marcus restless and in pain. I gave him his injection and left him with his parents while I joined the others in the garden. We made a circle and sent our love to him by praying for his spirit to be released from his body.

These last few months had seemed endless, so much pain, so much honesty and patience, as his physical body fell away. I came back inside to sit in Marcus's chair by the kitchen table and waited. Through the open doorway, his father stood beside the bed, stroked his arm and, although not a man prone to crying, openly wept. Years of a strained relationship now fully healed as he acknowledged his son's inner strength. I heard his father suggest he might call the minister. Marcus let out a low, deep guttural cry in disagreement. His father, quite overcome, then stepped outside to feed the dog while his mother went into the adjoining bathroom.

As I moved to his bedside, Marcus made some low, deep noises in his throat. I thought at first he was in pain, but then sensed something more, that he was trying to speak. I called his mother back into the room as Marcus called out more strongly. It was his goodbye. His entire face seemed to settle into a thousand tiny lines, his eyes momentarily shutting, then his face completely relaxed, his eyes opened again and a gentle smile spread across his face. I put my arm around his mother and whispered, 'I think he has gone.'

We waited maybe ten seconds, no breath. I called the others inside. His father held Marcus crying, 'He is still here.' But there was no pulse, just the sense of his spirit leaving his body. Maria, who had been sitting on the swing in the garden, said that she too felt the change, looked up and sensed his spirit leave.

Shortly afterwards, with perfect timing, friends Tara and David arrived, and David, a doctor, certified the death. We then bathed Marcus and dressed him in his tuxedo, placing written prayers under his clothes. We decorated his bed with flowers and silks, put crystals and treasures in his pockets, held each other, prayed, lit incense and candles. Finally, our beloved, brave friend was at peace.

The following day, as the funeral arrangements were being completed, many came to visit Marcus, including lots of children, who put notes in his pockets. They lay beside his body and openly asked those questions only children can ask, and were answered honestly and frankly, as we all felt they deserved the truth. The house filled with flowers and we kept his body cool with fans and chilled water bottles.

We held Marcus's funeral later that week under a huge fig tree in a local park. I had talked with my friend Pam about taping the service and as we tested the recorder, we suddenly heard Lama Zopa, the Buddhist monk and teacher saying 'This can be a great healing' and Marcus replying in a strong voice 'YES'. It felt as though he was back, reminding us that this was to be a celebration of his life.

My children picked bunches of flowers and gathered rose petals to scatter. They had both been very close to Marcus and loved him dearly. A table had been set up with cards so messages could be written to him, and these were then placed in an urn to be burnt with him. Later we found that my son had written many delightful messages with questions such as 'Is there chocolate up there?' and 'Can you see me, Marcus?'

Another table was laid with a silk cloth. A Buddha was placed there with candles, flowers and a board with photographs of Marcus through the years. His coffin rested high on a platform surrounded by flowers. The celebration included all the songs Marcus had requested. Maria and the girls danced with silk scarves. Poems were read. Many people spoke. Friends sang 'Amazing Grace'. Then at the conclusion we released balloons.

My eyes followed a pink balloon that was the last to disappear. So poignant as it was Marcus's favourite colour and the pink triangle is the symbol of the gay com-munity. Maria rang a bell as they took him away in the hearse to the crematorium.

Later that afternoon a lively wake was held in Marcus's garden, food having been delivered by the local restaurants. Curiously, that evening the ropes on the swing in the garden broke and the child who had been playing on it slipped gently to the ground. I went into his room but was overcome finding the bed empty. The reality of his leaving was now inescapable. I was in no mood for talking and took the children home to play. Leaving them with my housemate I walked to the top of our hill to watch the sunset, and be by myself and pray.

That night, after many days of drought, the rains came and with them my tears. I had been a small part of an extraordinary journey, one that was a great teaching in so many ways.

The following day, I had my university sociology exam. I was feeling apprehensive after the emotional strain and lack of preparation time, but was determined to attempt the exam. As I travelled down the main street of town, out of nowhere came a pink balloon! No-one was chasing it or paying the balloon any attention as it bumped across the road in front of my car and came to rest in the alleyway opposite. Tears smarted in my eyes and I called out, 'Okay Marcus, this better mean you are here to help me.'

When I reached the parish church where the exam was to be held, I was greeted at the door by the minister. He told me that my lecturer had rung ahead and asked him to support me. He led me into his office where a pot of tea and an open fire were waiting. I completed the three-hour exam in just two hours. When the results came through, I got a high distinction. Thank you Marcus. I can hear you laughing even now.

Laura Upsall

Photographs, poetry and fresh flowers make wonderful offerings.

Putting together
the ceremony

A funeral is a wonderful opportunity to honour and celebrate a life, regardless of the circumstances or timing of death. Even a stillborn baby with a life in utero has had a relationship with his or her parents.

Some like to have the funeral at a place of worship, a funeral chapel, a home or a hall, others prefer an outdoor setting—the choice is yours.

You can also choose a funeral celebrant, who will create and conduct the ceremony for you. It's useful to know that anyone, a family member or friend, can also be the celebrant.

Your choice of venue and service may depend on where you live. If you are in a city, outside locations can be tricky. City chapels are often booked and they have limited time slots. If you want a longer service, book two slots or book yours to be held at the end of the day to avoid feeling rushed.

There are many ways of honouring loved ones, such as in religious services with hymns and a eulogy, or a free-flowing service you have written yourselves. Whatever the service you can include music, eulogy, poems and speeches from a range of people, and you might like to consider an opportunity for spontaneous tributes during the ceremony.

As you put the service together, there are plenty of opportunities to involve friends and family. You could invite someone to sing or play a piece of music. You could ask others to put a compilation of music and visuals together in a multimedia presentation. This is a great way to involve teenagers, who may be more skilled in this area. Keep in mind people may want copies burnt on CD as a keepsake. The planning can stimulate stories and memories, as well as tears and laughter, and can really assist the grieving process before the funeral. Some love to have a favourite photo enlarged and displayed by the coffin on the day.

It's helpful to have a printed order of service so everyone knows what to expect and where they may be included such as in group singing. This can double as a thank-you to those who have been supportive and is something many people like to keep, so think about including photographs.

Decide ahead of time if the coffin will be carried into the venue, or whether it will already be there when everyone arrives. If you decide to have it carried, you can choose your own pallbearers, or the funeral director can provide them—remember, women can carry a coffin too.

You will need to decide on whether you'll have an open or closed coffin. Many families choose to have an open coffin so mementos can be placed inside. This is particularly comforting with children so they may be buried or cremated with their favourite toys.

If the coffin is closed it can still be adorned with flowers, candles, fabric or a large photo. Flowers from your garden can also add something more personal. The touches you can add are endless.

At one funeral each grandchild laid something on their grandfather's coffin to celebrate his many passions: a cricket bat for his love of the game, a World War II medal, a sheet of music as he was a gifted pianist, and a trowel to mark his love of gardening. The oldest introduced each child in turn and told a story about each object. At the funeral of a beloved grandmother, all the men wore pink ties, to honour her passion for pink. At another funeral a little boy put binoculars on his father's coffin so his father could look down and see him from heaven.

If the funeral is held outside or at the graveside, chairs should be provided as people will need to sit, and shade may also be something to consider. Sometimes people bring blankets and sit with their children as a family, allowing the time together to feel less formal. At the completion of a graveside ceremony it is customary to throw a little earth on the coffin or scatter flowers or petals over it.

Once the service is over you may want to invite everyone to attend the burial, if not a part of the funeral, or the wake. Make sure they have a clear idea of where the cemetery or venue is. It may help to have a few maps to give people.

A funeral often brings together family, friends and colleagues in a way we rarely experience in our daily lives. It is a precious time to be savoured and valued, not rushed. Many people want to linger together afterwards, laughing, crying and reminiscing as a way of coming to terms with the end of their loved one's physical life. Nowadays, this is generally the start of the wake.

A brilliant ending

Parampara and I had been friends for a long time. Over the years our paths were constantly interwoven. At times we saw each other, at other times we didn't. Then I got the phone call: 'Parampara has lung cancer, the prognosis is not good.'

I was shocked, I dreamt about her all night. They were not good dreams; the signs were ominous. I called her—she was scared. It was the nights she was finding most difficult.

She had always told me how important my music was to her and how healing she found it. Indeed, it was her support that led me to study music at university. I knew that there was a way I could help her in the dark hours of the night, when fear was at its worse and pain was acute.

I bought her an iPod and assembled a collection of my original music I felt would be calming and relaxing. I mixed these with other pieces which I knew were her favourites. It was a pink iPod; she loved pink. She also loved the music and it provided a sanctuary in those dark nights.

The weeks drifted past and I didn't hear from her. I had told her to contact me when she needed me. Then I got the call: 'I need you and want you here with me.'

As circumstances would have it, we were both in the same area. I had gone there to spend some weeks working on a music commission. I went over to her place. I was shocked at the demise of my darling friend who had been so full of the sun. Her body had withered away. She was on morphine, had gone through radiation and chemotherapy. Nothing had worked. She was in her last weeks. The end was near; all the signs were clear.

'What do you want to do?' I asked.

'Take me to the beach.' She had always loved the ocean, the sun, dolphins, anything to do with the beach. There was a storm brewing, the sky was grey but she didn't care, she so wanted to go. I packed her into the car and we went down to the place where the river meets the ocean. Her house had a track to the beach but she was too weak to walk the distance, so we went to a place where I could drive right up to the sand.

As we walked gently along the water's edge, the sky became darker with ominous clouds and she started talking to me about her funeral. 'I want you to be in charge of it, Yantra,' she said. 'I want you to create a celebration of my life, with music and sacred elements.'

A soft rain had started falling and I opened an umbrella above our heads, holding onto her with one arm, the umbrella with the other. She walked with a beautiful African shaman's walking stick, dignified, regal, fragile and frail. Thunder was rumbling and a storm was imminent.

Suddenly out of the skies a huge bolt of lightning cracked through the black clouds. The umbrella that I was holding had a steel frame. A high-tensile electric sound crackled through the steel umbrella frame as a deafening thunderclap enveloped us, accompanied by a blinding white light. We both fell to the ground with the impact. We lay there for a while, stunned and shaking, then we looked up at each other in shock, and started laughing and crying and laughing.

'I thought I was going to die of cancer, not a lightning bolt,' she said.

A surfer, who had been in the waves and saw what happened, came running out of the water to see if we were alright. He found us still laughing hysterically because we felt we had been 'saved' despite going through a such a powerful initiation together. I gathered her up and took her back to the car and we made our way home. We weren't sure what it meant but the experience had a profound effect on both of us.

That evening we were sitting together by candlelight and an owl flew to the window and looked in at her. Riveted, they held each other's gaze for at least ten minutes. The owl wasn't interested in me. It had come for her. Their communion was tangible.

We had many precious moments of stillness, sadness, joy and meditation together in the last days. I felt privileged to have been invited into her orbit at this challenging time. It was an honour to be there, to wash her, cook for her and be a friend to someone who was passing through the veils in such a brave and beautiful way.

My life has been enriched by the gift of sharing these last weeks with my dear friend. She taught me refined attention to detail and gratitude for the small things. All became intricately defined and took on a rarefied fragrance, one that exists between the worlds when one door is closing and another is opening, the moment between the breaths of in and out, the magical time of surrender and letting go. I have been given a glimpse of the beyond through the intimacy of shared moments with my dying friend.

No two people die the same or live the same. We are precious and unique jewels, each with a different song to sing and path to be walked. To share the harmony and the road at certain times of quickening makes the joy of life even more exquisite.

Yantra de Vilder

Taking care of the practical details

Where there's a death there are some very real and practical details to attend to. Being aware of the issues can help to make this transition as stress free as possible.

Often in relationships, families or businesses, financial matters are dealt with by one person. When this person dies it puts added pressure on partners, children, friends or family to undertake these responsibilities when they are feeling particularly low and vulnerable. It is not an easy time to learn new skills. So getting your affairs in order before you die can help and take the pressure off those left behind.

It's worth setting up an enduring power of attorney: This gives someone you trust the legal right to deal with the practical administration of your affairs, should you be unable to do so yourself. You can also create an enduring guardianship, which gives someone the right to make decisions about lifestyle and quality of life on your behalf, should you be incapacitated and unable to do this. It also helps to write an advance medical directive which maintains all your personal wishes for medical administration, such as a NFR (not for resuscitation) directive. These documents cease to be valid after death.

Writing a will stating how you want your assets distributed, your body dealt with and your funeral celebrated makes it easier for those left behind. It is common to choose two executors to share the load. Your executors hold the legal right to decide what will happen to your body and at the funeral, and to oversee financial issues. It's important they know where to find the will. Executors can be anyone: family members, friends, a solicitor or the public trustee. It would be naïve to say that issues do not arise, even in loving families—they do. The very nature of this sad time and experience shines light on issues that have been hidden. If everyone is able to approach this time with love, forgiveness and integrity, it can prove to be a time of great healing.

Will kits are readily available from post offices or newsagents. To die with no valid will is to die intestate. This then requires those left behind to apply to the courts for a grant of administration, where an administrator is appointed and organises the distribution of assets, giving priority, as required by law, to the surviving partner and children. These requirements will be dealt with by a solicitor if you choose to use one. In Trish's case, there was no will and limited possessions. However, there were a number of upstanding members of the community able to sign statutory declarations about her wishes. This helped to avoid the long delay it normally takes for the decision to go through the system. As everyone involved knew what Trish wanted, and with no animosity amongst family members, they worked together to honour her wishes.

To arrange a funeral there must be documented proof of death. In most cases doctors or hospitals provide this. If death is unexpected, causes unknown or the person has not seen a doctor in the past three months, this document may come through a coroner as an autopsy will have to take place. After the burial or cremation the death must be registered with the Registrar of Births, Deaths and Marriages. You must then apply for a registered death certificate which takes about a month to process.

If you have used a funeral director, they will organise this for you. Or you can do this yourself. The cremation or burial and the funeral arrangements can also be arranged without a funeral director.

If the assets exceed a certain value, then a grant of probate must be applied for. A solicitor usually does this, but probate kits are available if you wish to do it yourself. It helps to keep a certified copy of the death certificate with you at all times as you undertake financial requirements such as changing or closing bank accounts, insurance, superannuation, tax returns, your own will, credit cards, subscriptions, mortgage or rental agreements, child support, utilities such as gas, water, phones and electricity, council rates, vehicle ownership, health funds, government benefits and business details. Bank accounts are frozen at death and the only payments a bank will make from the deceased's account are for funeral expenses. After probate is granted the executor distributes the estate once all the debts have been paid. It can take three to six months for this to be finalised.

Accessing money from insurance and superannuation before or after someone has died can make a huge difference in the final amount of money received. Superannuation is for one's retirement, but in the case of premature death a lump sum may be paid to the deceased's family. Life insurance may or may not be paid out to the estate, depending upon the way the policy has been written.

It may not be necessary to spell out in detail exactly where your belongings go. A brother and two sisters experienced a powerful learning curve when they were required to divide up what their parents had left fairly amongst them. A couple of years prior they were each asked which items had particular sentimental value, and were gifted these at the time. With everything else their parents said they were to work it out amongst themselves after both parents had died. The siblings learnt to operate fairly and kindly with each other, determining what had greatest meaning to each and sharing accordingly. This method was great for strengthening their relationships, and a beautiful final gift from two very loving parents. They also decided they wanted their own children to have the same healthy experience.

Asking your children or family which items have particular sentimental value, or marking them with a sticker, or giving them away beforehand are also options. Make sure you ask your loved one these questions before they die and also about the entitlements of those who knew them well. Sometimes it can be advisable to put this into writing as confirmation of your wishes to avoid any uncertainty later.

These may seem an overwhelming amount of issues to deal with, but simply pace yourself. Remember when your brain can't function, it is one of the body's great coping mechanisms, allowing you to deal with only small amounts at a time. Although it may feel otherwise, you are not alone, so ask for both friendly and professional help. As time goes by, you are likely to look back with great pride at what you have learnt and dealt with at this time.

Till death do us party

Towards the end of the summer, I couldn't keep food down. I had lost 12 kilos. Scans showed an aggressive tumour in my oesophagus, which was malignant. It had invaded organs and tissues nearby.

The way the doctor and nurses said goodbye made me feel worried. Checking on the internet, I discovered this type of cancer was particularly virulent: only 9 per cent of people are cured. My doctor recommended surgery. The surgeon organised an appointment with the top surgeon. He checked my scans and said, 'I'm sorry, it's too difficult for me to guarantee to get it all. The operation would take six months to recover from, I wouldn't do it to you.' I was now very worried. Further tests led to my oncologist putting together a program of both chemo and radiation over a 27-day period. It was recommended that I didn't drive up and back for the treatment as it could lead to me dropping off to sleep on the freeway. It would take six weeks to be effective.

My partner Barbara had enough to deal with, so the wonderful local community rallied. After my plight appeared in the local press, good friends and people I had never met rang to offer their services as drivers.

The trips up and back suddenly became the only excitement I was to get in my strange new world. Radiation sessions didn't last long, the round trip for these would take less than three hours. The weekly chemo sessions took five hours.

The atmosphere in the chemo room was pretty tense. There were twenty chairs, pumps attached to cannulas, grim faces, all ages, some bald, some were business people on mobiles still trying to keep their busy lives on track. Some had their loving children beside them, obviously worried sick. Not much to laugh about. That was until one volunteer driver, my friend and Indian comedian Sandy Gandhi, arrived. She shook hands with everyone, saying, 'Hello, I'm Sandy, Australia's most easterly Indian!' Followed by some well-used joke. The atmosphere in the room changed immediately to one of good humour and healing which both staff and patients enjoyed. They all wanted Sandy back again.

I was still playing golf, despite the chemo pump I had to wear strapped to my waist. It was designed to pump every few minutes, 24/7, somewhat disconcerting at night when it was hard to find a comfortable position for the pack.

After all this effort scans showed the tumour was burnt to extinction, with just scar tissue left. The next six months were a time for celebration and maximum enjoyment. I felt I had cheated death.

However, some months later, a lump appeared on my throat. After a fine-needle biopsy, it was found to be malignant. My doctor looked at the results and said, 'Bugger, bugger, bugger, you are gone.' My oncologist pronounced that I had less than six months to live. I told him that I would go home and prove him wrong. My doctor put me in touch with another onco-logist who virtually said the same thing, only he put it more gently. He offered more chemo to 'prolong your life a bit', and arranged for me to have the chemo put into my arm at the local hospital. Cycling over there to receive it on a Saturday morning was fun. Within half an hour I was back at home, having experienced little or nothing from the injection. They obviously felt it was palliative.

Slowly the cancer spread throughout my lymphatic system, forming new growths called secondaries. The situation was looking pretty hopeless. This led to a flurry of activity. Friends arrived with health books, pills, liquids and alternative healing stuff. At a time like this you certainly learn who your real friends are.

When facing death, you realise for yourself there can be an acceptance of what is happening but it's the ones you leave behind who will suffer. I started to put my house in order and talk to my nearest and dearest about my beliefs and wishes. This was the hardest thing to do.

I decided I didn't want a funeral. I have no religion. I felt there was not one funeral I had attended which did true justice to the person. I decided I would like to be cremated and my ashes put on my dog's grave in my garden. I did, however, request a wake before I go. Barbara shared this idea with a few of her friends and they got really excited. It was decided to call this an 'Awakening', as by now, many people were openly discussing my death.

I was 70 years old, still playing golden oldies rugby, swimming, playing golf and politically active. People started to think 'If that bastard can die, what hope do we sedentary lot have?'

Once the news broke, I couldn't walk down the street without people asking me how I was. They seemed frightened to use the 'C' word. I usually responded, 'I'm not sick, I've just got cancer. I will be over it soon, please do come to my Awakening.'

Within a short time, three hundred $35 tickets were sold to my Awakening at my local golf club. The dress code was 'Come Heavenly'. People dressed as angels, devils, St Peter, even Jesus turned up, plus, inexplicably, a mermaid. In typical local style, 60 non-ticket-holders came, expecting to pay at the door. They all got in.

The club was packed, record takings were made. I was carried into the club by 'The Smoking Joints', my golden oldies rugby team, on a stretcher with my eyes closed. On the stage were images of the pearly gates with a sign that said 'No queue jumping'.

St Peter announced the evening's entertainment. A twelve-piece swing band put everyone in the right mood. Two beautiful girls in bikinis, one dressed as an angel, the other as a devil, did some erotic pole dancing. I was invited to dance with them and vie for their attention. I obliged. Local comedian Mandy Nolan gave me a roasting with her jokes. Other speakers got up to talk and I was worried they might make the night too serious. How wrong I was! [See page 238.]

I had decided to auction my souvenir rugby shirts. Mandy helped with this and in a few minutes we raised another $1000. Selling the story of the night to *That's Life* magazine raised a further $600. All up, the night made a profit of more than $6000. I am certain my favourite community group, the local youth service, will put this to good use.

I had already pledged a bequest of $20 000 to a memorial sub-fund. This was matched by other donations, which swiftly took the total up to $53 000. Having spent years of my life as a fundraiser, I appreciated this immensely. With gifts, bequests and pledges, a huge capital sum can then be invested to provide much-needed income from its earnings that is given as grants for active community groups. A committee will decide on the annual donations to go to successful applicants. A great idea well worth supporting.

My Awakening made me feel like a new man. I was walking on air for days. I cannot go down the street now without someone saying, 'Are you still here? I want my money back.' I love it.

It occurred to me when I was contemplating death, we are all dying. We never know when our time is up. Not long ago, just down the road, four young men laughing and joking one moment were dead the next. Their driver lost control and smashed into a tree. Life can be over that quickly.

My biggest problem facing my death was how to break the news to my daughter Emma who has Down's Syndrome. When her granny died in Canada, a lady she hardly knew, Emma was distraught and cried for weeks. During one of her visits, I showed Emma newspaper articles on my Awakening. She gradually understood. Now she prays for me. She has felt my confidence.

I realise now a great deal of healing is in the mind. If only the medical profession would accept this as fact and make it a friend, not the enemy. What's wrong with the placebo effect? This leads me to the reason why I am now on my fourth oncologist. I started at a regional hospital with a wonderful doctor. She suddenly disappeared. I was passed on to one of her colleagues; I didn't like his attitude. It was similar to his boss who told me so ungraciously that I had less than six months to live.

After this scary statement, my doctor arranged for me to see another specialist, who only used chemo. His efforts failed to halt the tumour in my neck, which grew at an alarming rate. The weak dose was probably my fault. I had expressed a wish to keep my hair and standard of living. I wanted to continue playing golf and enjoying life. My concern was that, when it was obvious the strength of chemo I was getting wasn't working, he only offered stronger chemo not radiation.

Then suddenly I found my original oncologist was back. She had suffered a breakdown and was now recovered. I was so relieved to see her return. Full of confidence, she looked at the latest CT scan and gave me hope that with radiation we might get rid of it. Well, I just skipped out of her rooms.

Looking at all the people in the waiting room, I wanted to shout, 'Don't trust your doctor, get lots of opinions!' I didn't of course, but my advice to you is always check around. The chemo guys have an arsenal of 50 different poisons. The radiation people cannot burn in some places twice.

In my opinion, I feel all patients are guinea pigs, helping to raise money for the hospital, and doctors have a problem accepting the possibility of spontaneous remission. They also seem to have difficulty understanding the importance of positive thought. Not enough unbiased work is done checking the effectiveness of alternative therapies. I feel certain there are many options open to the terminally ill. My advice to anyone is to take your diagnosis as an opportunity to grow, go for self-improvement.

My temper is now more under control. I still have problems making decisions about any activity further away than three months. It's hard keeping positive all the time, with a death sentence hanging over your head. I must try harder to believe that I can beat cancer. The prediction that I would eat less and less, sleep more and more, and then one day just not wake up is pretty attractive. There are far worse ways to go.

I've noticed some people get angry and ask 'Why me?' Others use their diagnosis as an opportunity to manipulate their loved ones, which is understandable, but not a good idea. I have always felt that one should 'aspire to inspire before you expire'.

When I look back over the last eighteen months, I feel I have done this. So many people have approached me and thanked me for things I was not aware of. The truth is that in our local community people are far more relaxed discussing death and dying now. Surely, this is a good thing to have inspired.

*

Zenith explains: Tony wrote this piece for us a couple of months before he died. I visited him a few days before his death. He was thin and gaunt, yet very dapper, up and dressed in jeans, black sweater and blazer, all set to go out, as always the man about town. As I sat with him, I could see his exhaustion and pain. His body was letting him down; his spirit, however, was indefatigable, many others would have been in bed or on the couch in loose comfy clothes.

I explained I could do the paperwork which would allow his body to go straight from his bed, to the box, to the car and into the cremator, that he didn't need a funeral director if he didn't want one. In this way, in one of his last actions he could buck the system and save a dollar, both causes that were close to his heart.

His wishes were clear. He didn't want anyone to see his body, nor have a funeral. He wanted to go alone to the crematorium with no fuss. He had written a letter for his daughter Emma, saying goodbye and telling her how much he loved her, making sure she knew he would always be there with her in spirit.

The following Sunday, Tony and Barbara were at a barbecue with four of their closest friends. Although weary, he was totally present. Tony had lunch, followed by plenty of chocolate. Later he started to vomit and haemorrhage. He spent about fifteen minutes in the bathroom with the two other men, then when the bleeding stopped, they all came out.

Paul offered Tony the choice of going to hospital or getting in the spa. In true Tony fashion he chose the spa. Patti, the hostess, had already phoned for an ambulance because Barbara was worried about how ill Tony looked. He was lifted into the spa, his head and body tenderly supported. Barbara noted how comfortable and peaceful he looked in the warm, scented water. His body appeared weightless, gently floating. As the men lifted him out, he took a few short breaths, and was gone.

Tony's was a beautiful water death in the arms of Barbara and his beloved friends. He would have been happy, dying, outside in nature peacefully and loved. Even Barbara felt happy because, despite his wishes and her commitment to support him, she had a dread of him dying at home, afraid she would have to deal with it all by herself. As it was, she too was surrounded by friends. They will always have that shared time as a special memory.

The ambulance took his body to the hospital to keep him cool overnight. On Monday morning I did the paperwork. Paul and Barry delivered the white cardboard coffin in Tony's own station wagon.

Between us we lifted Tony's body from the morgue drawer and placed it in his coffin, then put it in his car. One of the doctors needed to make a correction to the documents, so Paul and Barry went around the corner to Tony and Barbara's house, so she could say her last farewells. She chose not to see his body, because this was his wish and she wanted to remember him as he was.

This unexpected opportunity allowed several neighbours to pay their last respects and write loving messages in coloured texta on Tony's coffin while it was still in the car. Barry and Paul then set off to the crematorium, which was already expecting them, with Paul driving and Barry sitting in the back with his arm over the coffin. So it was that Tony departed on his last journey with his best mates to accompany him.

By this time Barry was starting to feel more comfortable, so he suggested they have a last beer together in a small town en route. Paul agreed but only if they could get an easy park. As they approached the pub, a car parked right outside pulled out and left, giving them the space. They went in and ordered three beers. When they told their story to the publican he said the drinks were on him.

They drove to the crematorium without further delay, holding a lively conversation about how good it felt to honour their mate and his last wishes. It was the simple, no-fuss ending that Tony had wanted.

When his ashes were collected later in the week, they were taken to two women who ran a funeral art business. They made a papier-mâché rugby ball to hold his ashes and painted it with local images and, expressly at Tony's instruction, the route of his pet project, the elusive but much-needed town bypass. It was a wonderful thing to behold, and overseeing all of the imagery was a large eye, looking down over everything, omnipresent, just as Tony had been in life.

Tony left instructions that he wanted a New Orleans–style funeral procession, with people dressed in colourful costumes and playing music, and that's what he got. Family and friends gathered, passing his ashes ball around, and then set off on the route of the bypass, ending up at the pub. The band played on and Tony's favourite singer, Lisa Hunt, belted out some great old hits while people danced and talked and ran with Tony's ball.

Tony's death was very public and didn't allow much space for sadness. Bravely and lovingly, his family and friends honoured his wishes fully while also dealing with their own loss.

The way Tony choreographed his death may not be for everyone but he raised a lot of awareness and money as a result of his approach. It has encouraged much more open discussion within the community. Tony's inspiration is ongoing as people now ponder the many ways in which to deal with death for themselves and their loved ones.

Tony Narracott   *Zenith Virago*

Organising the wake

Ireland is famous for its wakes, which traditionally were a time when family and friends literally 'stayed awake' to protect the body and keep a vigil before it was taken to the church for the funeral.

Today, as funeral directors usually take the body away as soon as they are called, the chance to sit with the body of a loved one at home has been lost. Wakes have become something that happens after the funeral as a form of celebration. As in a number of cultures, Maori people still observe this time with the body for up to three days—it is tremendously important in helping them express and acknowledge their grief. To sit with our dearly departed in the company of those we love is extremely beneficial for the recovery process. When extended family and friends gather from far afield, it can also be a chance to reminisce, and later distribute keepsakes or gifts. It may even be the last time such a gathering takes place, if the centre of a family or network has died.

When a sudden or accidental death occurs, especially to a younger person, a wake with the body before the funeral can be a more private opportunity to share the shock and other emotions, leading to an easier transition into the funeral. It can also be a time to contribute to the coming funeral, by making things together or encouraging people to share their memories.

Recently Jim, a surfer, died of a heart attack on his board in the ocean. His body was brought home the night before the funeral. His family and friends prepared a special place for him in the sitting room with photos and candles. What started in sorrow and a feeling of loss evolved through the evening, as they told stories and shared their feelings, into a memorable night. This shared intimacy continues to support them still—it was a perfect prelude to the small private funeral in their garden at home the following day.

Not all wakes are festive, some are solemn and don't include a place for lightness, but sharing food together gives nourishment after the intensity of the experience. As we will see in Arne's story, his wake was an evening gathering, held in the garden around a bonfire, ending with fireworks as a symbol of going off with a bang—a transformation by fire.

Casey recalls her mother's Irish wake. Kitty died at 97 and was laid out in their sitting room, looking as though she was about to rise up and sing and perform for everyone. She was dressed in one of her amazing glittery outfits, with gorgeous jewellery, make-up, nail varnish and lipstick—since the age of six she had been a singer, dancer and actress. The funeral director had tried to tie her hands together in the customary prayer position across her chest but they kept springing apart as though she was singing. For several days people came to the house in droves to pay their respects. It was a time of gaiety mixed with sadness, as people celebrated the life passed.

The idea of an 'Awakening' or a wake before you die is somewhat novel. Some people say they don't want to miss out on all the things said about them when they are dead and, like Tony, choose to have their wake ahead of time. The idea of celebrating with everyone you love reflects a fearless acceptance of your mortality which can have a profound effect on all present.

Celebrating the life of a loved one doesn't stop at the wake. On All Souls' Day, on 2 November, many believe it is easier for the souls of the departed to visit the living, so some cultures leave offerings of food on the table for them. Special altars may also be set up at home where photos of the deceased are placed, along with flowers, candles, and favourite foods and drink. This is a simple, easy and wonderful way to give thanks for all the gifts received from departed loved ones and for those people who have touched your life.

Another lovely tradition to honour loved ones who have passed over is to place Christmas wreaths on their graves. In Scandinavian countries on Christmas Eve after a carol service in the local church, people light the candles they have bought from those in the church, then take these outside in the snow, where they place them on the graves of loved ones, sometimes with a beautiful red poinsettia. This done, they return home to start their Christmas celebrations.

Mexican-style Day of the Dead celebrations have recently spread around the world. As many people no longer have the graves of loved ones to visit, it is becoming increasingly popular to create a day and a place where communities can gather to honour their dead.

In one local community this centres around an ancient fig tree beside the river, near a children's park. A coloured rope is wound around the tree and everyone is invited to peg their photographs and messages onto it. A community artist sets up a work table before the ceremony begins. Leaves, fabric, paper and clay are provided with which to make a message to or token for a loved one. People make boats from leaves, quilt squares and prayer flags from fabric, tablets and, of course, hearts from clay, and write messages, letters or poems on coloured paper.

Candles, messages and the clay pieces are placed among the gnarled tree roots. Added to these are photographs, lanterns and boxes containing the ashes of loved ones, even pets, making the entire tree a beautiful organic shrine. Later, a ceremony is held to celebrate everyone's individual and collective loss, after which people come to the microphone to share their stories and to remember their loved ones by name.

The messages are then either left on the tree, burnt in a fire or buried under the roots of a sapling tree, or the leaf boats floated down the river to the sea. A local choir encourages everyone to sing and many people stay on to be with one another afterwards. People are at different stages in their grief, but all are consoled by not feeling alone in their loss. This community event touches and bonds everyone in the intimacy of sharing their stories together.

This re-introduction of the Day of the Dead is growing and is becoming a vital part of many communities, and hopefully in years to come people will stay and share a joyful picnic together on the grass in a way that has happened for centuries. In so doing they will be honouring their dead in a creative and supportive environment.

Remember your loved ones for years to come.

Caring for my ex-husband

Ifound it hard to accept Arne's brain was deteriorating. I didn't want to believe he was dying, even though I knew in my heart he was. He'd always been so full of life. Now he looked pathetically thin, bones poking through his fragile skin, eyes sunken in their sockets and such an air of hopelessness.

Arne and I had been divorced for five years. Since his diagnosis of cirrhosis of the liver, our two sons—Kai, fourteen, and Roland, nine—had lived full-time with me. Arne was alone. The rest of his family lived in Sweden. Despite this, Arne insisted on staying at home. Community nurses came several times a week. He had Meals on Wheels delivered, and Homecare sent someone every day to wash him.

I was desperately worried but I didn't want to live with him. I felt quite panicky as I thought of the future without Arne. I was angry. Arne had brought this on himself.

As our children had been born at home it seemed logical to believe in the idea of a home death. So, here was the reality. I had to face it, or at least give it my best shot. But without my sisters I don't think I could have faced it.

During that last Christmas of Arne's illness, my three sisters and their families had come to visit. On New Year's Day Arne suddenly went downhill. He could barely walk to the table. He wasn't able to hold his fork. I tried to feed him, but even when he had food in his mouth he wasn't able to swallow. It was terribly distressing. Later I got used to it, but that first day it was very hard to watch. By the following day we were looking after Arne full-time.

Arne slipped into a coma with only brief periods of consciousness. I wasn't sure if he knew he was dying. I didn't want him to miss the opportunity to let us know his last wishes. During a short period of lucidity I asked him if he realised. There was a long pause. 'Yes,' he said. He could barely speak.

'I think it will be quite soon. Is there anything you want to say to the children?' I asked.

There was another long pause. 'Not yet.'

'I think you'd better do it while you still can.'

But he'd drifted away again. I didn't think he'd be with us much longer.

The nights were long, with me waking up every two hours to roll him over and massage him. It was like having a baby again. He couldn't chew, so the nurses suggested giving him powdered food that he could suck through a straw. Once we did that he picked up quite dramatically and was much more conscious again. He was more able to move about in bed and sometimes even stood up and walked a few steps.

I wanted to ask Arne what he was thinking, what it was like to be dying, but he couldn't speak much. There was no way he could articulate complex feelings and emotions. He didn't seem scared and he wasn't in pain. He just seemed to drift off somewhere else.

Kai said to me one day, 'I'm confused. I thought Arne was dying and now he doesn't seem to be.' It certainly had looked as if he was going to die but Arne was always a teaser. There was no way he was going to miss out on the fun of having my family around. I asked him once if he wanted visitors. He said no. 'But what about all my family?' I asked.

'Oh that's different,' he said, smiling.

We heard of the Amitayus Hospice Service through friends. It's a volunteer organisation that cares for dying people in their homes. I was pretty desperate because my sisters couldn't stay forever and I was buckling under the strain. Not that Arne was difficult, but caring for someone full-time is very demanding, not to mention seven children between us in the school holidays. Everybody who came from Amitayus had a special quality, such willingness to help and such concern and compassion not only for Arne but for all of us.

So many people were generous. I was immensely grateful for any help. Even a few hours in the daytime so I could do the shopping or return to my house and mow the lawn. Some Amitayus volunteers stayed overnight.

We kept a diary that anyone could write in. It was a way to express some of the confusing and conflicting emotions of this time and to remember stories of Arne. It was a comfort to me to read and re-read things people said about him.

Looking back, Merryn, an Amitayus carer, wrote: 'In hospital, death is very often seen as the enemy, as failure. I have often felt that medicine has fought for a life that was freely being surrendered. In Arne's case there seems no fight—only peaceful acceptance. Is that why there is no pain? Being a volunteer is an interesting role. Not the nurse, no uniform to hide behind, not family, no definite place in all this. And yet we are all family on a deeper level. It's good for me not to have a traditional role to play and just accept the feelings that I have, both of love, responsibility and yet detachment.'

There came a time when my sisters couldn't stay any longer, so sadly I had to let them go. It was very quiet with everyone gone. Arne seemed sad after they left, but cheered up when an old friend dropped in.

The thought of looking after Arne indefinitely, maybe for months, with this level of care, was overwhelming. I wanted to help him die peacefully at home, but I didn't want to live with him as such. So I decided to commit myself to the next two weeks, then reassess, to do it cheerfully, or otherwise there was no point doing it at all. I felt a lot better having made that decision.

The children were unbelievably patient with Arne. He used to call them repeatedly and they always came. They had hardly left the room when he would call them again. Sometimes he didn't really want anything, just them.

Kai's diary entry recalls: 'Death, it's usually taken so seriously and makes everybody feel sad. I always had it in the back of my mind Arne wouldn't live long. Yet here we are trying to be serious and meaningful and he keeps stuffing around and making jokes. I keep expecting Arne to tell me some wise last words or something important. Yet Arne taught me quite a lot without meaning to. I have learnt patience from his lack of speed and movement. He taught me that if you want something badly enough you can get it, because he built the big beautiful house he lives in (even though he was an ageing man who wasn't particularly smart or strong). He also taught me leadership and responsibility because from about the age of twelve I was the man of the house who made the final decisions and got Rolly and Arne to bed on time. He taught me never to give up on myself.'

I often needed Kai's strength to hold Arne up while I cleaned him, or to get him back into bed if he fell out, which he sometimes did. It was hard for the children to see Arne like that. I hoped I was doing the right thing. I thought it was probably better for them to actually be able to do something to help him, to do things our own way, without feeling helpless as one does in hospital. Life continued around him, with kids, animals and friends coming and going.

In the last two weeks before Arne died I was numb, a strange feeling of detachment, waiting, doing things for Arne with almost no feeling. Then, after talking to one of the carers,

I opened up again and all the pain came rushing in. I felt so sad for Arne, this wasn't how I wanted it to be. I was beginning to fear his death, fear the hole it would leave in me. I met Arne when I was twenty. That's 21 years of knowing him. Life without Arne seemed unimaginable. I wondered if it would liberate me from my feelings of responsibility. I think I wept for our lost relationship as much as for his death. Would the pain of our separation never stop?

Arne hung on for Roland's eleventh birthday and it was a nice day for him. Arne ate watermelon, a mistake as he couldn't chew it, and chocolate cake which he liked. He appeared less aware of life around him. He knew it was Roland's birthday but seemed confused when I brought in presents.

The last day was so difficult to watch. Arne was different somehow. I'd never seen death before, but I sensed it. His words were muddled. His breathing was getting harder, such a struggle, gasping for air, with so little room to fit it in.

At one point Kai said to me, 'This is terrible, why doesn't he just die?'

His face seemed to have changed shape completely. He could no longer even suck water from a straw, so I tipped it into his mouth with a spoon. His eyes were rolled up in his head. I asked him if he was ready to go yet, but he shook his head violently and looked really panicky. Roland came and sat with him and cried. Kai also sat with him much of that day.

When I was alone with him, I told him how much I loved him, had always loved him, how kind he'd always been and generous, and how I'd always felt safe with him. He seemed to understand and his eyes caught mine for a moment.

Later, with Kai and Roland there, I very gently told him it was time to go. I said, 'It's time to go now Arne. We all love you very much but it's time to go. We will be alright without you. You have suffered enough and now it's time to go.'

By this stage Arne's breathing was quieter but weaker. About 11 p.m. I decided to go to bed for a while, leaving my friend

Marguerite with him. I went to sleep. Soon Marguerite called me urgently. I rushed in as Arne was taking his last breaths. He was vomiting, it was like black coffee. I wish I could say that it was peaceful but I can't. He had a look of intense horror on his face. Marguerite threw the cat off his bed and we rolled him on his side. I held his hand and wished him a safe journey. We thought he was dead and Marguerite asked if we should clean him up. Just then he gave another convulsion. It was about midnight but I don't think there was an exact moment when he died, because we could feel his heart beating faintly for quite a while after he stopped breathing.

I felt sad but relieved that it was over. It was peaceful in the room. Kitty was asleep on his bed again, and the other cat asleep on the sofa. Eventually I lay on the sofa too and dozed a bit.

About 6 a.m. I heard the boys waking so I went upstairs. Roland jumped up, asking, 'Is he still here?'

'No,' I said, and Roland flopped back onto the bed. 'But his body is downstairs and you can come and see him if you want to, but you don't have to.'

On seeing Arne, Roland showed no fear or distress. I said it was okay to touch him and Kai gave him quite a hard poke on the cheek. I gradually rang people, and some came to visit and say goodbye. When I look back on that day, I think of it as a truly beautiful, peaceful day. We played him music, lit candles and brought flowers. Everyone seemed happy and sad at the same time.

I didn't ring the funeral director until the afternoon and we arranged for Arne to be picked up the next morning. I felt I wanted one more night with him. I slept in the opposite room from Arne and was comforted to know he was there, although this time he wouldn't be calling me.

At the funeral we wanted to carry the coffin ourselves. It was very heavy but we managed. There were flowers everywhere and the chapel looked lovely. I had desperately wanted to see the coffin go into the furnace. This had never been requested before, but they arranged it for me. The coffin was high on a trolley. The attendant opened the furnace and I felt a blast of heat and saw the red glow. He pushed the coffin in and turned a wheel to close the door. Then he turned up the heat.

It was a very powerful moment. I felt triumphant and complete. I felt like tearing down the wall of the chapel so that everyone could see the coffin going into the furnace. I wondered why some people want to hide from reality. I had to see it. I didn't want to spend the rest of my life wondering what they did behind those curtains. I know they burnt Arne's body because I saw it.

I came back to the chapel and, crying, said, 'Now I know he's safe.'

For the ashes ceremony Kai and Roland had wanted much more of a celebration than the funeral had been. They wanted something wilder and more fun, something to capture the spirit of Arne and his viking ancestors. They asked for fireworks. It was quite a job procuring them, with special permissions from the Lands Department and Fire Department, but finally it was arranged.

In the days after Arne died a lot of people rang and sent cards—all saying nice things about Arne, in the hope of comforting us. However, this had the reverse effect on Kai, who became angry. It made me realise that it was important to acknowledge the less pleasant side of Arne, for Kai's sake, as he was the one who'd borne the brunt of Arne's anger. I asked Zenith if she would take this into account in her eulogy for Arne, which she did beautifully.

'I used to argue with Arne a lot,' Kai recalls. 'He was an aggravating old bastard, but I loved him, and it was only when he was sick and dying that I remembered what the real Arne was like, and not the drunken hermit. The real Arne was interesting to talk to, funny and warm.'

Roland had his own memories: 'Arne was my loving, gentle and kind father who has gone to that mysterious place, up or down. I hope Arne is safe and happy wherever he might be. It was nice living with Arne, because he didn't mind what we did. We were allowed to bicycle and rollerblade in the house, and we would sometimes surf down the stairs on mattresses.'

The following Saturday we had our ceremony. We built a big bonfire. Lots of people came with their children. We all took a pinch of Arne's ashes and spread out around the garden to scatter them. As I gazed back at the house looking so beautiful, I thought of all the people who cared for Arne and loved him and I was filled with anger.

It was a hard moment and I just wanted to stay there in the darkness and cry, but as the hostess I felt I'd better go back. Everyone was around the fire chanting:

May the longtime sun shine upon you,
All love surround you,
And the pure light within you
Guide your way home.

There were lots of ashes left so I picked up the bowl and walked around the fire, letting them pour through my fingers like sand. I found Kai in the darkness and Roland too, and we did it together. The chanting stopped and there was silence.

Then suddenly, spontaneously, a man called Peter gave a great roar and running, leapt over the fire. It was awe-inspiring. Someone shouted Kai's name so he ran and leapt. Then I heard my name. I gasped. The fire was huge! But I too ran and leapt— what a feeling, so uplifting. Then Roland jumped. Everyone had a go. Afterwards I went up to Peter and hugged him. He was shaking with emotion.

My sister and I donned our fireman's gear, a friend was put in charge of crowd control, and we set the fireworks off. It was very exciting! They were huge and very loud. After that we shared food and sat around talking, looking at old photos and gazing into the fire.

The ashes ceremony was a very special night for Kai and Roland. Next morning Kai said he felt satisfied. I felt it too. We did everything we could to give Arne a great send-off.

At the ceremony Annette, a close friend, sang a beautiful song in Swedish that touched me deeply.

Who can sail without wind? Who can row without oars?
Who can say goodbye to a friend without tears?
I can sail without wind. I can row without oars.
But I cannot say goodbye to a friend without crying.

Harriett Clutterbuck

Caring for the carers

Whether caring for a partner, family member or being part of a team caring for a friend, it's important not to forget that all carers need some tender loving care themselves, to recharge their own batteries. It's helpful to take walks, reflect, write and have quiet time, so if you're a carer you need to commit to nurturing yourself as well as allowing yourself to be cared for by others.

While nursing Trish her family accessed a carers' support program through their local neighbourhood centre on the advice of the aged-care officer at council. Once a week Richard listened to the carers without judgement, allowing the carers to talk about everything they needed to talk about openly. This in turn gave them the strength and courage to continue. Without these sessions they may not have given Trish what she wanted, or survived the process of caring for Trish to the end.

Most hospice centres also offer respite care to carers when they need time out to attend to other family requirements; or should they be exhausted or sick themselves, they will give the patient a bed for as long as needed.

Carers who are focused on supporting the one they love to die a painless, loving death and who need to administer medication can find themselves in a difficult position. With all the debates on euthanasia and instances of people self-medicating with illegal drugs, the carer's actions could be open to questioning. This is why the support and encouragement of the palliative care doctors and nurses can be so important in making carers feel safe and acknowledged in the active role they are taking. Professional advice can be invaluable in helping deal with pain management and the comfort of loved ones.

Carers may also feel that what they do is scrutinised by others close to the loved one. This can be daunting. Patience and sensitivity can help a great deal. Jenny was nursing her partner at home after a diagnosis of less than three weeks to live. His sisters were concerned about the quantity of morphine and sedatives in the house, and asked her 'What if someone accuses you of killing him?'

Knowing she needed to focus entirely on nursing her partner, Jenny chose not to ask herself 'What if I do something wrong?', although she understood their concern. 'They were feeling overwhelmed by everything, but I didn't dare go there,' she says. 'It had only been a couple of weeks since they received his call to tell them he was dying. I found it required even more of me, knowing that I needed to support them and consider their needs. After all, this was their little brother who was dying. I felt a strong need for them to trust me, and I knew I had to prove that I was trustworthy.'

With so many separations and new partnerships these days, children and young adults often share loyalties between parents and step-parents. Past relationship difficulties may still be very raw. With a need to focus completely on the dying person's requirements, situations can occur where people can feel pushed aside or disregarded. Dying lifts the lid on unresolved issues, and great sensitivity and awareness are required to deal with this. It is almost as if a spotlight is shone into the darkest corners and every possible emotion will arise. Although death brings great opportunities for healing, nerves may need soothing, and it often falls to the carers to encourage others to resolve painful past experiences. Knowing this can happen helps avoid reactions that might add further pain.

When visiting a dying person, take the opportunity to stay a little longer and have a cup of tea with their carer. Encourage them to share with you aspects of their life spent with the person who is dying. Look at photos to reminisce and relive the beauty of their time together. Support them to discuss old hurts and unresolved issues, as it may be too late for them to talk with their loved one about these. Carers often experience a heightened sense of awareness in the constant company of the dying. They feel, sense and see much more than most. Give them an outlet to talk about these experiences. It can be a sacred time for them, and you as well.

Those who are dying are our teachers, not the other way around. As a carer this calls for great humility. It becomes apparent that permission is often needed to allow the dying person to leave. Even if they are on the edge of death they may remain for a long while if someone is not letting them go. It is important, especially for children, to give permission for parents to go. As a carer you may need to let children, and others, know that, while also assuring the dying person that everyone will be looked after when they have gone.

After death it is essential to stay in touch with the carer. For them the loss can be so vivid it is almost as though a part of their own body has been ripped away. As Jenny says, 'Your life disappears when they die, because you also lose your plans, dreams and future.'

The emptiness in a carer's life can be palpable when the many details surrounding death are dealt with and everyone else has returned to a normal routine. Six to eight weeks later can be a particularly lonely time, when outside support is crucial. Carers often long for the company of those who have recently faced the same experience. It can be helpful to link them up with others to talk through the memories and details of their experience. Carers rarely receive their deserved acclaim, yet they are life's angels and need to be treated as such.

Losing a young father and husband

My husband Peter died of a brain tumour at 37. Peter and I were very happily married and the proud parents of two beautiful children, Chloe, six, and Dylan, three. We first knew something was amiss with Peter's health two years before he died, when he suffered a grand mal seizure in the middle of the night. We almost lost him then.

Peter was not an epileptic, so while he lay in a controlled coma a whole battery of tests were run. Many things were ruled out but nothing came back conclusive. The diagnosis was made based on an MRI that had shown a lesion in his left temporal lobe. We were told Peter should slowly improve over several weeks and should have a full recovery.

So when the neurologist looked at the second scan a month later and said, 'I am sorry, there is no way to soften bad news—you have a brain tumour', my world caved in. Shock and disbelief gripped my body. The walls of the doctor's office seemed to tilt into odd angles. I remember my breath coming in short gasps, while I tried to stifle the wail that wanted to rise up and spill out.

Peter seemed so calm. He asked logical questions. My mind

reeled but I somehow managed to find my centre enough to pay attention and ask questions too.

A biopsy was quickly arranged. It was bad news. Peter's prognosis at the time of the original biopsy was two to three years. An even bigger shock wave hit me. I felt as if I couldn't possibly survive my despair during those first few days.

In retrospect I see my grief started there, but the journey of terminal illness is not linear. Peter and I both collapsed into his death sentence for about a week. Then we came up fighting for Peter's life. In Peter's words, 'We must fight with all our strength to save my life as this is the path we tread and we must tread it totally. The battle is joined, but there are no losers.'

Peter asked me to focus on the research, the practicalities of running family life and his medical schedule, so that he could go inward and be with his mental, emotional and spiritual self. Peter's spiritual life was rich though not easily defined. When he was a child he spent four years with his family in an ashram in India. He used to say that he was grateful to have had loving parents who 'dropped out' in search of a spiritual path, and who encouraged him to embrace personal growth.

When he looked inward in those early weeks, he said: 'For me, the experience is a revelation. I am stripped down to what is important and everything else is trivial. I have no resentment or anger, only a certainty that all is for a reason. I trust that. Jennifer and I both sense that. Whether I survive is unknown, but I know that I am here to increase love, and to learn and grow. That I am willing do so at any cost, even to death. I trust this is the beginning of a new, more direct way of fulfilling my purpose. I am a vessel, not a victim, and this is the sea I chose to sail before I was born. The tumour is a tool, a means to an end. There are no accidents. I can see that this experience increases love. I have no regrets, although I dearly want to see my kids grow up and to grow old with Jennifer. I will fight until I win or it is time to let go.'

How could this be happening to our children? Chloe was four years old and Dylan was only fourteen months when Peter became ill. Peter was a wonderful loving father, playful and fun. I wondered how deeply this would scar them, to lose their beloved papa at such young ages?

At the time of Peter's diagnosis I spoke with Chloe's school teacher about how to approach the subject with Chloe. She suggested telling her in story form, keeping it in a beautiful light but being honest. I agreed. But when I sat with it I did not feel as though it was the time to tell her that her father was dying. I thought it might be possible to find an alternative cure, and even if we didn't he would probably live for at least a couple of years. Telling her Peter was dying might cause her undue stress. I chose to focus on what was actually happening in the moment. The changes in our family needed to be named and my frequent tears needed some explanation. So I said, 'Our family life is different since Papa got ill and went to the hospital, isn't it?'

Chloe replied, 'Yes it is, you spend much more time with Papa now and not so much with me and Dylan.'

'How do you feel about that?' I asked.

'Sad,' Chloe admitted.

'I feel sad too,' I told her. 'Sometimes I cry. I cry because I can't play with you and Dylan as much right now and because Papa can't do all the things he used to do like go to work and drive the car.' I let her know I was always available to talk about what was happening. She crawled in my lap and had a big cuddle, then was off playing again. Describing what was happening in our family life seemed to be helpful to her.

At that point I felt sure our integral approach would surely save Peter's life. Maybe other people died from this disease, but Peter wouldn't. He wasn't going to be a statistic. We would find a way to save him. Besides, he had always lived a healthy lifestyle, was a non-smoker, very moderate with alcohol, surfed and ate organic food.

While we engaged with the most up-to-date conventional medicine we also embraced a myriad of alternative approaches. Diet, supplements, a naturopath, a homeopath, an acupuncturist, an Aboriginal healer, an ex-scientist from NASA who had cured himself of leukemia, a medical intuitive, long-distance healing from John of God in Brazil, and emotional release work. Much healing was offered, but it did not cure Peter's body.

Almost two years after Peter's initial seizure, the door of Peter's hospital room opened bringing me out of my musings. The director of the palliative care services, a kind and gifted physician, took me aside and said that when she looked at Peter she saw a very sick man. She knew Peter and I wanted him to die at home. She felt we should get home as soon as possible, because if we waited over the weekend he might not be able to make the one-hour journey.

Five days later Peter died at home surrounded by many loved ones. It started early in the morning. Peter was in our bedroom in a hospital bed and I had a small bed near him. I heard Peter stirring before dawn. I got up to see what he needed. He was almost completely paralysed at this point. We had to change his positions to keep him comfortable. It was the last time I saw my beloved husband with his eyes open. He looked at me but did not speak, did not respond to my enquiries. He just looked. I knew something was disturbing him. I felt helpless, not knowing for sure what it was.

If I had known that was the last time I would see Peter with his eyes open, I might have lingered. The look in his eyes is indelibly imprinted in my mind.

Peter had recently had a cough, as did all of us in the house. Up till this moment his lungs had remained strong enough to clear his secretions. I noted now that he was not clearing them.

Sometime later the household began to awaken. Peter's mother and my mother were staying with us. After breakfast the children wanted to go to the library. I knew I couldn't let them leave the house without saying a final goodbye to their papa. He might die while they were out.

I had someone bring them into the room. Dylan immediately said, 'Why is Papa gurgling?' I explained that Papa's breath was changing because this was the day he was going to die, the day he was going to take off his 'earth coat' and go on an amazing journey. We had talked about this previously.

Dylan became distressed in my arms and cried out, 'I don't want Papa to die!' He twisted his body this way and that, repeating 'I don't want Papa to die' over and over. I started sobbing. This was heartbreaking for me. I was already completely devastated to lose my lover, best friend and husband. To watch my children have their hearts broken too, and to stand by helplessly, was the most excruciatingly painful experience.

I am told I had a beautiful exchange with Dylan at Peter's bedside. I don't remember what we said, I was in too much shock. I only recall at some point Dylan got out of my arms and walked to Peter's bedside table. On it were photos and other symbolic items. Dylan chose a beeswax rainbow that Chloe had made for Peter and a flat, turquoise stone. He walked purposefully to Peter's side, tucked the items into the crook of Peter's arm, reached up on his tiptoes and kissed Peter's arm, then climbed back into my embrace. He was still squirming and whimpering, but clearly had found a way to say goodbye.

All the while Chloe sat in Peter's mother's lap and watched, with her chin tucked down, looking very uncomfortable and distraught, saying nothing. Before leaving the room Chloe kissed Peter on the cheek, for the last time.

One afternoon, ten days prior to Peter's death, Chloe, Peter and I had a magical conversation on his bed. Golden sunlight flooded our room. We spoke of how things were. Chloe was able to hear that Peter was not afraid of dying. She understood he did not want to die, because he wanted to live with us, but he wasn't afraid. We also spoke about what we would do with Peter's ashes. Chloe had clear and strong ideas about it. It felt connected and healthy. She had such a good cuddle with Peter. He even managed to pull faces at her and make her laugh. After a while Dylan joined in, and we took our last family photos with Peter.

After their final goodbyes with their papa the children had different needs. Dylan wanted to stay home and be near what was happening. Chloe clearly still wanted to go to the library. I think for Chloe she could deal better with what was happening with some space and quiet. Both children were supported in what was right for them, and for that I am grateful.

I stayed by Peter's side all through the morning. His breathing was very loud and laborious. I was beside myself, wondering if he was suffering. I felt devastated yet acutely aware, in a heightened and altered state. I was focused completely on Peter.

As midday approached, Dylan needed his afternoon nap. I snuggled into the curve of Peter's neck and whispered to him. I let him know I would be out of the room for a few minutes, and I would understand if he needed to go before I was back, but that if he wanted to wait for me I would be back soon.

When I came back, a couple of friends were in the room with Peter. I settled back in with him. I let him know I was there and that I loved him dearly. I encouraged him to let go, and head for the light. A marked change happened then. His breath came with longer and longer gaps in between. I sent someone to get Peter's mother. She came back and several others followed. The gaps increased, his chest still heaving with every breath. Then they became impossibly long. Every nerve fibre in my body was firing intensely yet I also felt centred in the moment there with Peter. He breathed out his last breath. I don't know how much time passed before I knew no other breath was coming. When I realised he was gone I let out a wail from somewhere inside myself, from a depth I had never experienced, ancient and primal. I collapsed by his side and wailed, and wailed, and wailed.

Dylan, Chloe and I spent time with Peter's body that evening. Dylan had a lot of questions: 'Can Papa talk?', 'Can Papa eat dinner?', 'How will he pee now?' I let Dylan lead the conversation and was willing to go where he needed to go.

Chloe was quiet, but seemed calmer and more relaxed than she had been in the morning. When I finally tucked the children into bed, out of the darkness came Chloe's sweet voice. 'Love never dies,' she said.

We kept Peter's body at home through the evening and overnight. Sleeping near him that night was both comforting and peaceful. I woke up often and though devastated I was amazed at the serenity in the room. Peter was no longer suffering.

The next morning close friends and family members arrived to help me wash Peter's body, shave him and anoint him with lavender oil. We played beautiful music, lit candles and went about our work with a feeling of reverence and open-heartedness. Our children and friends' children moved in and out of the room. The energy was similar to being in the home of a recent birth.

In fact, being with Peter through his death reminded me of being with a woman in labour. I felt like Peter's midwife. It seemed as if he were birthing himself out of his physical body into a new realm.

Our friend Zenith had given me all the information to prepare me and let me know our options surrounding Peter's death, months before he died. She continued to guide us in the days to follow and give invaluable support. She held our family and community through Peter's home-funeral celebration. We were in shock, living through the tragedy of losing Peter so young, but also feeling a sense of satisfaction that we were able to care for him and fulfil his wishes. I have no regrets around Peter's death and funeral celebration and for that I am so grateful.

In my eulogy for Peter, I said:

My beloved Peter, we took the fast track and covered a lot of ground in the past eight years as a couple. It is impossible to believe you are really gone. My heart has a deep ache and my body yearns to embrace you. I feel your love present in me. You have lived well and there is no doubt that you fulfilled your mission in this life . . . You HAVE increased the love in the world. You will live in my heart forever, for you are my dear one.

I began to keep a grief journal, to document my experience and particularly my children's journey, about three and a half months after Peter died.

*

Today I took Peter's name off the car insurance policy. What a strange mixture of feelings. On the one hand I am feeling pleased with myself that I managed to accomplish another business task (it helps that the kids are out of the house). On the other hand it feels so strange, so wrong, as if I am casting him away, erasing him out of life. How can this be? I feel as if I am doing him wrong, letting him slip into oblivion. It has been three months and two weeks since Peter died. My mind still cannot totally believe the finality of his parting. I must remember this void I am in is teeming with possibility: in it live past, present and future. I must not dismiss the feelings I have and the intense grief but must feel them and stay connected to life. I am being stretched and grown by life. A poem by Rainer Maria Rilke comes to mind about fighting with an angel and how what we fight with is so little and what fights with us so great; I am trying to surrender to trusting that I am being shaped by that angel, by life.

Dylan and Chloe are pretending to be penguins this morning. They watched *March of the Penguins* recently. Dylan said to me, 'I am a dying penguin. I am very old and I am dying in the snow. The snow is covering me up now.' He swayed and in slow motion, fell onto the sofa and covered himself with pillows. Dylan told Chloe he wanted her to 'come and kiss him because she loved him sooo much'. Then he said, 'I will become a butterfly after I go back to Mother Earth. And then I will be a little moth.'

This intrigued me because Elizabeth Kubler Ross talked of the butterfly as a repetitive symbol for hundreds of dying patients. I know Rudolf Steiner also used the caterpillar, cocoon, butterfly progression as a way of indirectly supporting young children in their understanding of the death process. We have a beautifully illustrated children's story about becoming a butterfly that I often read to the children before and after Peter's death.

I remember as they watched *March of the Penguins* being worried that the scene of a dying penguin who got lost away from the flock in the snow would be upsetting for them so soon after Peter's death. In fact, nature and the movie gave them a good playacting role to further assimilate and understand this mystery phenomenon that has been so powerfully a part of our lives these last six months.

I went to a concert of sacred music the other night. One song especially touched my grief. One of the lines was, 'My life is in your hands'. I thought of Peter and how he had trusted me to care for him. His life was indeed in my hands. This knowledge and experience touch me in a place I find hard to articulate. Ours was an incredible intimacy prior to his illness and it only deepened when he became ill. I felt tears slip down my cheeks and a hollowness in my belly. I miss him so.

I had a cry this morning about my struggles with Dylan. He is pushing the boundaries so frequently and I feel I am on him much of the time. It isn't much fun. In fact, it is quite exhausting. I wondered whether it would be this way if Peter were here. Certainly he would be sharing the parenting and limit setting. I am worried I could be squashing Dylan's masculinity. He is a boy being raised by a mother and older sister. Perhaps he'll grow up to be great with women or rebel against them. I called my friend Ursula who assured me her three-year-old daughter is acting in much the same way. Perhaps it is a developmental thing. I hope so.

It is now four months since Peter died. I feel less of the constant intensity of grief these past ten days or so. I also feel more lightness coming in and a sense that my future is going to be fantastic, different from my wonderful life with Peter, but also really good.

I still have moments of intensity which I think will be with me for a long time. Yesterday I was looking for something on the computer and I came across photos of Peter a few hours after he died. I sobbed when I saw them. It feels good when I do cry. It is an acknowledgement of my loss, and afterwards I feel like a blade of grass swaying in the breeze after a cleansing rain.

Dylan seemed so tender this afternoon. When I cuddled him in his bed he went to sleep quickly. I lingered to smell him and feel his soft cheek. I gave that tender little cheek a few extra kisses tonight. It hurts him not to have his papa and that starts both my grief flowing again and a desire to meet a wonderful new partner and father for my children. It is strange to feel both feelings at once.

A few days ago in the office at Chloe's school, a very out-there seven-year-old acquaintance called out to Chloe very loudly, 'Your father died!' Chloe sort of shrank next to me and made a murmuring sound. I said, 'Yes, he did.' I felt sorry for my kids. The little girl was brash and it felt so abrasive, but I think she was just inquisitive. She said, 'Do you miss him?' Chloe didn't want to speak and the school admin person looking after the girl whisked her away to some imagined task.

Later when I asked Chloe how that had been for her, she said she didn't mind really, but I did. I wanted to protect them from those abrasive feelings. I felt intruded upon. Perhaps Chloe knew the girl was just being herself and didn't expect anything else from her. I support talking about Peter and his death, but I prefer the circumstances to be gentle and respectful. Like when six-year-old Declan said to Chloe, 'It's really sad your dad died.' He said it in an empathetic voice, and Chloe opened up and spoke with him about Peter and her grandfather Roger's death.

This morning Dylan asked why I am using Papa's coffee mug. I said I like having my morning tea in it because it reminds me of how much I love Papa and how much he loved and still loves us. Dylan then asked, 'Will you marry Papa again, and then he can move again?'

I said, 'Do you mean could I marry him again, and then would he be alive again?'

'Yes,' said Dylan.

'Oh, I wish it worked that way sweetheart. But no, Papa won't be alive in that body that we knew Papa in. His body is dead forever, but his spirit is alive and his love for us will always be with us.'

'But how will I have a papa then? We don't have a papa,' he said tearily.

'No, you don't have a papa right now. But we have each other and I will take good care of you. No-one will ever be able to be just like your papa but one day you may have another dad...'

Before I finished he said, 'I want MY papa.'

'I understand. It is sad. I really understand.'

What more could I say? It is difficult enough at 41 to make sense of what has happened to our family. Imagine having your family turned upside-down at the age of fourteen months, and then having your father die two weeks after you turn three. This will mark Dylan for his whole life. I can only do my best and focus on the love that surrounds us. I hold the possibility for the children that Peter's death strengthens the children's connection to themselves and life rather than damages them.

Dylan gave himself concussion a few days ago. I spiralled back into shock for a couple of days. Being in the emergency ward with him, and knowing all the nurses, was confronting. I felt very alone in my parenting. The experience showed me my nerves are frail at the moment. I still need time to regenerate my reserves.

Since Peter died I am particularly anxious about Chloe and Dylan's wellbeing. I know now what it is to lose one so precious.

I don't think I could survive losing Chloe or Dylan. I try to be compassionate with myself when the anxiety arises. I try not to let it get in the way of Chloe and Dylan engaging in life in a normal and healthy way. Sometimes I simply have to name the anxiety to a friend and find a way to be gentle with myself.

Today Dylan said with sadness in his voice, 'I want to tell something to Papa. I want to tell him I love him.'

I said, 'All you need to do is say "Papa" and then tell him. He'll hear you.'

'But I want to hear him say something back,' he said.

Chloe then said, 'Just listen inside your head and he'll say something to you.'

Dylan smiled and said, 'He said, "I love you."'

Later that evening I wanted to check in with Chloe. She doesn't really talk about her grief and doesn't have all the questions that Dylan has about Peter's death. Chloe seems fine but I really don't know if it is because she is fine or because she's pushing down tough feelings. I don't want to make a problem where there isn't one but I am just not sure. I asked her how it is for her with Papa gone? 'Hard,' she said.

'How do you feel?' I asked.

'Sad,' she said.

I asked her if she knew it was okay to feel sad and okay to show she is sad? 'Yes,' she said. I explained that sometimes I worry I am so busy being sad that she may think I need all the sad space and feel like she can't have sad space. 'No,' she said, 'I don't feel that way. Mostly I get so busy playing I forget to be sad.' I am satisfied she is in an appropriate place with her grief for her age.

A few days before Chloe's seventh birthday, I became overwhelmingly lethargic. My energy was so low I could barely make it through the day. The next day was the same and internally I was beating myself up for being depressed, not being on top of things. I felt like a loser. At some point I said to a friend, 'I don't know what is wrong with me, maybe it has something to do with Chloe's birthday coming up.' I burst into tears, realising that it was my grief and feeling overwhelmed about Chloe having her first birthday without her papa that was getting me so down. It would be the first birthday where I didn't have my beloved by my side for our firstborn's birthday.

At least I understood why I had been so down. Gradually my energy began to pick up and Chloe ended up having a fun and sweet birthday even though her papa was missing.

Four days later came my birthday. I was squirming through the days leading up to it. A couple of friends asked about my plans and I realised that what I wanted to do was avoid the whole damn thing. I didn't want to face my first birthday without Peter. The night before I went to bed crying and the morning of my birthday I woke up crying. Making breakfast for the kids, crying. Making Chloe's school lunch, crying. I had to wear dark glasses when I took Chloe to school because I was like a leaky tap. I just couldn't stop crying.

At one point during the day while I was crying, I thought what a full experience I am having of being human. This brought an intensely beautiful wave of gratitude and sense of understanding about this journey called 'my life'. I felt so grateful I could cry and feel the hot, salty tears, feel the heaviness, emptiness and fullness in my heart, feel my love for Peter and the sense of loss, accentuating all that I had shared with him. I had so much with him, including this intimate experience of one of the most important moments in his life, his death. I am wondrously rich with experience. I am a human being. I can feel. Thank you life. Thank you Peter.

Jennifer Lalor

Helping our children
with grief

As well as feeling your own pain when a loved one dies, there's the pain and empathy and bewilderment of the children to handle. How do we deal with death with our children, especially if it's the death of someone close to them, such as their parent, brother, sister or friend. It's tempting to try to shield children from the pain of loss by excluding them from the experience of death. Many people think it is best for children not to see the body of the deceased, or even participate in their funeral. While this comes from the best intentions, it may actually do more harm than good.

It's important children are included in the process, and are treated with care and honesty. Keeping children away from death is robbing them of the opportunity to understand death and the precious memories it brings. Excluding them can cause lasting confusion, hurt and resentment.

Like adults, children also need to say goodbye to someone special, and to have a sense of completion. Just like us, they can only do this when they have the opportunity to be involved, and this includes visiting and being with the body of their loved one.

Research shows that allowing a child to be involved in the death offers them the opportunity to say goodbye in a tangible way. When they can honour the special person and relationship they shared, and express their feelings of loss and grief, it helps start the healing process, allowing them to adjust to the changes brought about by the loss.

When Jennifer's children suffered the sudden loss of their energetic and fun-loving grandfather, with Zenith's guidance they chose to create their own funeral. Roger was cherished in his community and many young children, along with Chloe, his three-year-old granddaughter, loved him. During the ceremony his body was laid out on a flat board rather than in a coffin, covered in silk, surrounded by flowers and placed on the floor to be easily accessible.

Young children aged between two and five helped place flowers around the man they remembered as a playful friend. They touched his face, felt his hands, then moved to a nearby table where they made drawings for him. The drawings were then placed with him in his coffin. As a result the children had the opportunity to discover for themselves that he was definitely dead, what 'dead' felt like, and to say goodbye through their drawings. Their parents felt this was a healthy approach to death and bereavement.

Through their families and community, children need to learn about life and death. They often have an innate feeling for these natural life rhythms, and benefit from sensitive guidance, as they come to terms with the impermanence of life. Exposing them to animal deaths, for instance, as they occur can be an easier way for them to experience the reality of death. When we gently stay close to them, and allow them to be part of the process, children often lead us to where they need support by asking questions, by expressing their feelings and through their actions.

Most children will ask questions and it's important we attempt to answer them as honestly as possible, in an age-appropriate manner. They need to ask questions so they don't get caught in their own imagination, making the situation worse or more gruesome than it actually is. Our explanations need to be simple and include hands-on experience where possible. Words are often not enough to understand what death really means for a young child. Sensory experience helps a child integrate the reality of death. As one child commented: 'We know Grandma is dead because when a person is dead her heart doesn't beat anymore. Our hearts are beating.' We might respond, 'Let's feel our hearts. Now let's feel Grandma's chest together? Do you feel her heart beating?'

It's also important never to force a child to participate if they seem uncomfortable. Our job is simply to hold the door open for their exploration, making suggestions and listening carefully for clues as to how to help them through the experience.

Many emotions arise for children around death. It's fairly common for children to imagine they caused the death of a loved one, talking of feelings of guilt. A child who has lived in a home with a family member with a long terminal illness may think they are 'bad' because of the relief they feel when that family member dies. Older children may not want to ask questions for fear their concerns are selfish, even though they may be wondering 'Who will take care of me now?', 'Will there be enough money for new clothes?' or 'Will I have a new mum or dad?' Young children may say they want the loved one to live but don't feel sad, like the grieving adults around them. When a loved one is dead, children need to know their feelings are perfectly normal. Grief counsellors can be enormously helpful at this time.

Children respond well to creating artwork, as art allows children to express what they may not have words for. A painting or drawing allows release of pain, and gives them the opportunity to say what they loved about the special person.

Art can also help bridge the gap in how life is changing without that person around anymore. As adults it is wisest to limit our responses to the artwork children make at the time of a death to questions about the artwork itself. This approach helps the child put words to their experience and tell their story, without adult interpretations. Good questions to ask include 'What is this shape doing?', 'Does your drawing have a name?', 'If your drawing could speak, what would it say?' or 'Tell me about the colours here'.

It can also be really useful to have a favourite aunt or uncle, or family friend, for the children to talk and play with. Some may not want to burden a grieving parent with their questions or needs, but may speak openly with an adult they trust. Children can have intense feelings one moment, and are off playing the next. This is both normal and healthy. Play gives children the chance to 'step out' and 'work out' what is happening in their worlds.

It's easy to forget children are important members of their families and communities and bring gifts to the death and dying process even though they are so young. Their viewpoint may also help others involved, as children are often simple and natural and even more accepting in their approach to death. When an elderly man died, his grandchildren asked if they could write the eulogy. As it turned out this was a gift to the family. Unbeknown to the children, two of his sons had very different opinions on their father's ceremony. The children, aged between four and sixteen, went off for a few hours on their own and all of them contributed to the writing. They presented the eulogy together and family and friends cried and laughed, touched by the memories, thoughts and feelings the children expressed.

It's a helpless, heart-wrenching feeling to watch a child lose a loved one. We can best serve our children by allowing them to be a part of what's happening by accepting their feelings, answering questions sensitively and honestly according to their age, and gently listening to them while loving them all the way through, however long that takes. When children can embrace death as a natural part of life, it helps them to grow into emotionally rich and healthy adults.

*Children's artwork allows them to express what they may not
have words for.*

Suddenly she was gone

Sylvia was my dearest friend. She was many things to me—a mother, sister and spiritual companion. Sylvia was in her early 50s, in excellent health and happily married with two teenage daughters, Sarah, eighteen, and Louise, twenty. They were a loving and close family.

Then early one morning while Richard, her husband, went to the shop to get milk, Sylvia was in the garden doing her daily yoga practice. Sarah was at the kitchen sink. Suddenly, she saw her mother on the ground. Sylvia had suffered a massive brain haemorrhage and died almost immediately. In distress and panic they called the ambulance, hoping against hope she could be revived. The paramedics tried to restart her heart, but Sylvia was clearly dead.

Eventually her body was taken away and Richard and Sarah, although distraught, rang me to let me know. I was deeply shocked when I received the news, and my partner drove me straight to their house. As I looked out through the car windows and took in the world, I somehow knew my life would never be the same. The house felt surreal and empty, a new and disorientating experience. Although I was in shock, I was very aware of the moment. I wanted to experience it fully, with as much understanding of life and death as possible. This was a woman I loved, with whom I had shared my heart, and who had been a treasured mentor. Her sudden death was a profoundly life-changing experience for me, but I had no idea then of just how much it would influence my life in the years to come.

Sylvia had a much-loved and wonderful family, all of whom were also my friends. After her body had been taken away, they were left in shock and disbelief. They telephoned friends and family. Unfortunately Louise, their eldest daughter, was overseas visiting her mother's family.

Later that afternoon Richard and Sarah had to go to the hospital to identify Sylvia's body for the police, which is the usual procedure with sudden death. They asked me if I would like to go too, so I could see Sylvia's body for myself. I thought that seeing her body would allow me to accept the reality of her death, and I was touched and grateful that they considered me close enough to share this experience with them.

We went to the hospital and were taken to the morgue by two police officers. As Sylvia's body was wheeled out on a trolley, the police tactfully looked away, trying to give us some privacy at this difficult moment. Sarah cried and Richard embraced her, while I looked at Sylvia and tried to take it all in. She was a big, healthy woman who looked so peaceful she could almost have been asleep, although the back of her head was a dark purple from the congealed and settled blood of the haemorrhage. My shocked mind was reluctant to accept what my eyes were seeing. Somehow I expected her to breathe.

This was my first experience with a dead body. As I looked down at her I said out loud, 'Oh Sylvia, I just can't believe this', and shook my head. Gently I started stroking her hair, from her forehead down over her crown. I let my hand gradually rest on her crown, as I would with a sick child, lost in my thoughts and emotions and deep sense of disbelief.

What happened then was one of the most extraordinary experiences of my life. I saw a column of energy leaving the crown of Sylvia's head. It passed through my palm and out through the back of my hand. It was palpable. It appeared as physical matter like a jet of vapour and had a force of its own, which continued up my arm and down to my heart.

Time stood still. I glanced at the police who were looking away. Then I looked at Richard and Sarah to check whether they could see what was happening, but they were immersed in their comforting embrace. I remember wanting to fully appreciate what was happening, knowing that it was something wild and very special.

When it eventually stopped, I took my hand away and stared transfixed at Sylvia's body. I was overwhelmed with the intensity of the experience. However, I needed to support Sarah and Richard, caught up in their grief and in all that lay ahead.

Back at the house, I offered to help them organise the funeral. It felt important for us to do it ourselves. I knew that wherever Sylvia's spirit was, she would be thinking, 'If Zenith's involved, it will all be alright!'

On the way home I drove through a small town and saw the new tiny office of a funeral director, which I hadn't noticed before. It was squeezed between an antique shop and the fire station. I went in and met Ron, and told him my best friend had just died, that I worked in a legal firm and wanted to undertake her funeral myself. I asked him if he would guide me through the process. In half an hour, he had explained the whole legal procedure, the forms and possible pitfalls. Ron was a generous and caring man. He gave his advice and time freely. He even offered to be there in the background in case anything went wrong. I gratefully accepted his offer.

I went into action. Richard was busy supporting Sarah and Louise, who was trying to organise a flight home as soon as possible. Sarah was still in total shock. A friend built a simple coffin, I did the paperwork with the coroner, then organised to collect Sylvia's body from the hospital morgue. Here I met some resistance, as this was new to them, but I was determined and not to be stopped. Sudden death requires the body to undergo an autopsy, so I had rung the hospital several times to explain that we were having an open coffin for absent family to view her, and asked them to do a tidy job.

We took Sylvia's body to a friend's house where six women friends washed and dressed her. The hospital staff had done their work well and we only had to clean up the blood around the stitching.

The friend who built the coffin became very emotional and was unable to finish it, so we found ourselves frantically stapling in a favourite fabric to line it with, before her body could be gently placed inside. The coffin was decorated with Sylvia's own artwork.

When all was finally ready, we lifted Sylvia in her beautiful coffin into the van, only to find we couldn't close the back door. The coffin was a little bit too long for the space. We took out the van's back seat and now the coffin fitted. Then I checked the petrol gauge, nearly empty. One of the women sat with the coffin for the journey to the service station, and on to Richard and Sylvia's house where Sarah and Louise were waiting with friends for the arrival of Sylvia's body. This time was particularly important for Louise who needed the opportunity to experience her loss on her own with her mother.

Richard's deeply spiritual outlook supported him through this challenging time, while also giving him the strength to support his grieving daughters. They were grateful to be able to spend a couple of hours at home with Sylvia before we headed to the crematorium for the ceremony.

The funeral was held in the crematorium gardens where more than two hundred people gathered. I was also to be the celebrant. I had never done anything like this before. I stood there in front of everyone, ready to begin reading what the family and I had written. I took in the scene, I felt so sad.

Taking a deep breath I calmed myself and from my deepest, most steady place I began the ceremony. Many people had asked to speak and sing, and I had a sense of order about how it would unfold. We talked, sang, cried, shared and laughed. We honoured her individually and collectively. Then at the end we let her body go.

I felt a great sense of achievement. It was also my 36th birthday, it had been an amazing day. I looked across and saw Ron, the funeral director, and bowed my head to him in gratitude and completion. He had stood in the background at the hospital, at the house of preparation, at the house of viewing and at the ceremony. He had not been needed but his presence had been supportive. Ron had been my guiding angel and with his generosity he had set me on my path. I felt exhausted but very satisfied.

I have now been involved with hundreds of people in death and dying, in many different situations. Ron's example to me has been a guiding force; it taught me that when someone asks you for information, to always give it with generosity, as you never know what they will do with it. I always carry Sylvia in my heart and because of my love for her, many people have experienced meaningful and appropriate rites of passage, ones that fully support the bereaved. It has been and continues to be an extraordinary learning, and a very privileged journey.

Zenith Virago

Spending time with the body

Spending time with the body is an extremely personal decision. For some it is natural to want to sit with the body for a while after death, whether they have been there up to this point or not. It's important to allow yourself and others this opportunity before you call the funeral director, as they will usually come and remove the body as soon as they are called. If the death occurs at home, you may decide to keep the body overnight. There's no need to rush things. Allow yourself the space to fully accept this death in a deep and peaceful way.

Where family are coming from overseas, spending time with the body is often doubly important, as distance can cause a great sense of separation. 'When my mother died in England, her funeral was postponed for three weeks until my sister and I could be there,' Claire explains. 'The day before the funeral we went to see her body for the last time. For me this felt like a very natural thing to do, even though I was very aware that her spirit was long gone, I knew she would always reside in me. Seeing her physical body lying there allowed me to focus on all the gifts she had given me in her life.

'I wanted my mother to be buried with a few special things she had so treasured. From an early age she had instilled in her three children a deep love and respect for nature. I had brought with me a kookaburra feather, a symbol of the laughing call which greets the dawn in Australia, and a reminder of her love of birds. There were also shells from the beaches she had always loved and a cascade of roses from the garden she had nurtured and worked in for as long as I can remember. It was a profound moment as memories flooded over me. I felt a deep gratitude for a mother who had always put the needs of her children ahead of her own.'

Many people feel the need to be with the physical body to realise the life force or spirit is gone. It also helps to give a sense of closure. People often say how surprised they are at how peaceful their loved one's face has become without pain. If family and friends have not been part of the dying process, it's important to warn them that they may find the deterioration shocking, and that they should be prepared for this.

If you have never seen a dead body before, you may have a natural reluctance. However, with someone there for support, you may be very glad you did. There's an alchemy that happens between you and your deceased loved one which is tangible and powerful.

There are others who feel strongly that they would prefer to remember their loved ones as they were in life, and do not want the face of death as their last memory. Some people feel that if the person was a private person in life, they would not want to be viewed in death.

In the case of sudden death, accident or crime, a family member will be required to attend the morgue with the police to formally identify the body. This is a very challenging situation and should be handled with great sensitivity, as the person is generally in shock and disbelief. The choice of who is best equipped to do this is a personal matter for the family.

To determine the cause of death there will need to be an autopsy or post-mortem, especially if there has been a recent operation or the deceased has not seen a doctor in the last three months. This is an invasive procedure, which sometimes can reveal an unexpected cause of death. It involves an incision from behind one ear, across the top of the brow to the other ear, then down the torso to the top of the pubic area. In some cases a more localised autopsy may be done. Afterwards the body is stitched or stapled up and prepared for viewing if required. Clearly, for many people this may be too distressing. If you are worried about the state of the body, it's advisable to ask the hospital or morgue for details on what you may expect or, in extreme cases, to ask someone close to do it for you.

For others, no matter the condition of the physical body, viewing it helps them to see that the essence of their loved one no longer resides there, and this too is important.

Ultimately, it's a personal decision, there is no right and wrong. Allow yourself to do whatever you feel most comfortable with.

Lost at sea

Flying is how my relationship with Will began. My daughter arranged for him to take me for a flight in his ultralight. I loved it, so he kept on inviting me. He took risks, but well-calculated ones, until the day of the crash. Eyewitness reports said he did a barrel roll under a thousand feet, but this makes no sense. It's not something he would do.

Three days before the accident I had gone to Melbourne for my son Tim's birthday. At first I was disappointed Will wasn't coming. The last time we spoke was the evening before the crash. I told him I was happy he had stayed home after all, as his son Joel had come to visit from overseas. They had resolved their past differences. 'I've got my son back,' he said. 'Joel's taking me on an adventure tomorrow, and he won't say what it is.' He was so excited.

The next evening I got a phone call to say they were dead. 'You're kidding!' I said, when my sister told me. 'You're kidding.' I couldn't think of anything else to say.

Joel's surprise had been a sky jump. Elated from the experience, Will took Joel for a flight. The ultralight crashed into the sea.

A week of bad weather hampered rescue efforts. Finding nothing, the navy search was called off. That time was very difficult for everyone. For Joel's mother and sister, their loss and pain engulfed them. Joel's body eventually washed up a month later. While we were all sensitive to each other, I was not a part of their grief nor they a part of mine.

After hearing of the accident friends and family gathered on the beach every day while the search continued. My house was filled with people caring for me, doing everything that needed to be done.

I walked the beach. I beat the waves as I stood in the ocean, then I would let it caress me as if it was Will's embrace. We had walked the tidelines together while I collected treasures from the sea, driftwood, shells and old shoes. It was something I had done since childhood, and Will shared in my delight. I was very aware of the irony of my walking the tideline looking for his body.

Will and I shared a love of the ocean. Will taught me to sail. We bought a sailing boat and sailed up the coast. We often spoke about how, when we were old, we wanted our bodies to be lost at sea when we died. We also spoke of needing to live a long time to make up for the time it had taken us to find each other, as neither of us wanted to grieve the other. We had talked of making preparations to die together when we felt too tired to live anymore.

While I kept telling people Will didn't want to be found, the consequences—legal or emotional—of not finding his body had not dawned on me. Maybe it was my way of keeping him alive. If there was no body, there was no proof that he was really dead. I knew Will would have wanted the sea to keep his body.

The words I spoke to Will were very different, as I raged and expressed my anger, distress and longing: 'Grief is like the ocean that took you from me!'

I was caught up in a violent storm of emotions during the first weeks following Will's death. The huge waves of emotional pain and despair swamped me, picked me up and hurled me onto imaginary razor-sharp rocks, shredding every cell of my body as they sucked me back into the depths of my being, into the deepest part of the ocean.

In that deepest part of myself I found a profound stillness that strengthened and nurtured me, preparing me for the next wave that would hurl me back onto the rocks. I learnt quickly that there was no use resisting this unpredictable process. Remaining focused on my breath made me less resistant. Painful as it was, I knew it wasn't going to kill me—but it was gouging great crevices through me. There were moments when I thought I wanted to die, so as not to face the years ahead without him, but I also knew there was so much I wanted to live for.

I began practising a Buddhist meditation in which I breathed in my own pain as well as the pain of those I didn't know but knew to be suffering. The Pakistan earthquake had just happened. Tens of thousands, cold and hungry, were grieving for friends and family. Their lives had turned to rubble.

Grief connects us to all humanity. I was not alone in my grief. I also had the love and support of many who kept me close and fed me.

Slowly, ever so slowly, the storm subsided. There was more time between the waves. They were also less violent. But my deep stillness wasn't always easy to achieve. I now had to work for it. My mind often took me into the 'What if?' and 'What now?' and 'If only'. Thoughts can be like quicksand taking us into their own story, making everything about me, I and mine. I don't believe life is personal. It just happens. We can make it mean whatever we choose.

In the first weeks I thought I could find a way to make Will's death not true.

I tried to squeeze myself through the fabric of time. I didn't cancel his phone for four months. I wasn't the only one who would ring just to hear his voice. It was even longer before I cancelled his credit cards, so as to keep alive the possibility of his return.

I continued to walk the beach, waiting for Will's body to be washed back to me. I wanted to find it. I didn't want anyone else to find it. Then, suddenly, I felt I couldn't wait any longer. I had to go on a journey. I needed to get away from everything that was familiar. It was five weeks since the accident. But the day I left I felt as though I was deserting him.

I don't know why but I felt compelled to walk in the mountains. I needed to go to the highest place. Jinki, my daughter, travelled with me to Mt Kosciusko. We tried to walk to the summit, but the wind and rain were too strong for us. I lost myself in the dripping, mist-shrouded mountains. Further south we drove through dead forest, still recovering from the fires three years before. The landscape reflected my grief. It absorbed me, made me a part of itself, part of all life, where life and death, destruction and regrowth, are a natural part of the landscape.

We visited family and friends, sharing our pain and joy at having known someone whose departure had left such emptiness in our lives. Will was larger than life. He held a strong presence in people's lives. For me, living a year with Will was like a lifetime with someone else.

I returned home and still Will's body had not come back to shore. I walked the beach again—always looking for his body. I didn't know how many pieces his body would be in. I don't know if not having a body made it harder to accept that Will was dead, but I noticed that I started to feel envious of people who were able to say goodbye to their loved one.

What a gift it must be to be able to ritually acknowledge everything you meant to each other and had shared between you. How soothing to be able to hold the body of your loved one, once they had died. I had kept one of Will's T-shirts that held his scent, until it eventually smelt mouldy. I consoled myself with knowing that the last words between us had been 'I love you'.

For a long time I don't know if I made sense—conversations had no real meaning but I still engaged in them to prove to others that I was normal. I would look at people on the street and wonder who had grieved, who was still grieving. I would find myself telling strangers that my husband had died recently. I still do. I don't choose who I tell it to. It just comes out. I find I've spoken before I know it. Just to hear the words out loud and to have them witnessed so that I know it's true.

Then, eleven weeks after the accident, Will's unidentifiable and incomplete body was washed up after a storm. I had been on the beach that morning, but further north. It felt wrong that I wasn't the one to have found his body. Three beach walkers found it. At first, they didn't know what it was. They called the police who called the council, thinking it was a sheep. The walkers insisted the remains were human, so finally an ambulance was called.

I was grateful that one of the people who found the body was prepared to speak to me, to tell me how it had been, where it had lain. I wanted to hear everything he could tell me about finding it. It didn't feel gruesome. It was information that was vital to me.

Perversely, I think Will would have liked the idea of his body being taken to the council dump. He would have liked my not having to pay all those over-priced funeral costs. It was another ten weeks before the forensic report was able to verify it was Will's body and he could be cremated.

I kept asking the police for photos of the body. I was dissuaded by everyone who felt it would be best not to see them. But I continued to ask for them all the same. They didn't become available until after Will's remains had been returned, by which time my need to see them had gone.

At the funeral parlour, I sat with his body wrapped in plastic, and felt his form. I wanted so much to be able to bundle him onto my lap and rock him in my arms. I wanted to rip off the plastic and feel him. I wanted to transform the stink of decay back into the warm scent of his living flesh. At the crematorium I watched his body burn. I wanted to put my hand into the fire and stroke his bones; I now fully understand why people will go to any length to recover the body of a loved one. From time to time I still look for his leg, feet, bits of his skull, pieces that might still be out there tossing around in the ocean.

I live my life more fully these days. I love life, yet am less attached. I am more content and less concerned by everything. The aching for Will is a part of who I am now. It doesn't diminish me. Crying is not a bad thing. Aching isn't a bad thing. It is just a part of my life.

Will died. That's just what happened. I was able to love him and be loved by him for eight amazing years. For that I am grateful. Not to be grieving him would be not to have known and loved him the way I did. That would indeed have been a sad thing. A year later, there are still rogue waves that catch me unaware.

Jill Trevillian

When you don't have a body to grieve over

While many people find a dead body confronting, when there isn't a body it can be even more traumatic, leading to disbelief and an inability or unwillingness to acknowledge or accept the death. These days, with extreme sports, mountain climbing and travel in more remote areas, losing someone without a trace is becoming much more common. Victims of crime are often in a similar situation. It may take months or years to accept a loved one's death, and as a result it may leave a lasting trauma.

It's natural for human beings to want to live in hope. This can often override the sad reality of a situation. In such circumstances families need even more compassion and care. To be held and supported by friends and community help the bereaved not to feel so alone in their terrible shock and grief. Support can be a lifeline during the initial agonising waiting for news. This is especially poignant when young children are missing and there's no proof of their death. In these cases in particular, a parent's imagination often creates conflicting realities. In the case of abduction or missing persons, families often live in hope for years.

Where there is no body to grieve over, the questions seem endless. Not surprisingly, people feel utterly desolate and unable to cope with their daily lives. Some people feel they need to escape, to avoid all the daily reminders of the missing person within their home environment. Time spent quietly in nature can help to ease the sense of hopelessness and despair.

One of the hardest emotions at this time is the feeling of powerlessness, so anything that can be done to help someone shift their attention from the missing body to how important that person was to everyone is very valuable.

After a period of time, it may be helpful to hold a ceremony or gathering to start to come to terms with the situation. Whether it is a small private memorial ceremony or a larger public gathering, it can be an enormous help for the bereaved who have been living in limbo. As everyone comes together to remember this loved one, they can acknowledge the situation, celebrate their memories, and support the family of the missing person. When finally feelings of emptiness and helplessness can be openly acknowledged, it helps to start heal the pain.

Others may not feel ready for this; some fear that by holding a ceremony they are giving up hope, even though there may be no hope. Professional counselling can be very helpful in gently supporting people to live with this situation.

Never coming home
from work

Some days life delivers things so unexpected that one feels transported into another, perhaps parallel, world. The 6th March was such a day. My son Aaron phoned me to tell me there had been an accident. Pete, who both my sons were working for that day doing contract tree surgery, had been killed. His head had been cut off.

I felt shocked to my core. I couldn't take it in. I felt overwhelming panic that my boys were in the middle of this. Aaron told me they really needed us there with them; his brother was particularly traumatised.

As we drove to collect them I couldn't stop my mind from wandering. At work they use chainsaws and ropes dealing with huge trees, logs, and limbs. What on earth could have happened? Confused, I found myself imagining many scenarios to make sense of it all but in retrospect I realise the subconscious has a powerful way of feeding us only as much as we can deal with at any one time. Not only were my sons working together, but also another young man whose family were thousands of miles away and who often stayed at our place. Three people would need our support; I had to get my mind functioning properly.

And what about Pete's wife and children? I didn't even know if he had any children. How could this have happened? Had Pete suffered? What trauma would his fellow workers suffer? So many questions.

Arriving at a little back street we saw Aaron's small tip truck parked by the side of the road. My eldest son, and their friend, sat on the grass, heads down, feet in the gutter. Aaron, a little further down on the other side of the street, was talking to the police. Distraught and wanting to be gone, the two boys hastily loaded chainsaws, ropes, helmets and gear into the boot of our car.

Walking down to meet Aaron, I asked the police what else was needed. Statements had been given and the truck was to be taken away for examination. They weren't sure if it was a motor vehicle or work place accident. The police seemed concerned the boys needed to go home. As we were leaving they mentioned evidence might be needed at a coroner's inquest, sometime in the future. A coroner's court? This was too surreal for this quiet leafy road on a beautiful sunny afternoon.

Reading the police statements at home we learnt what happened. Aaron's truck was used to pull out trees and foliage from the difficult access site using ropes and pulleys. An observer, needed to signal the driver on this job, was a woman, a family friend of Pete's. Observers always stand far away from any rope set-up as it could operate like a guillotine should it give way.

A brand new 80-metre-long, thick, nylon rope was used to pull trees from the bottom of the gully to where the truck was. Set up first thing in the morning, the system seemed to be working fine when there was a loud snapping sound. Aaron stayed in his truck, knowing what he had seen, but on hearing the observer's scream for help my eldest son raced up the hill, and straight inside the roped area where Pete's body lay. In an instant Pete's life had gone. Everyone was utterly shocked.

When a work cover representative arrived, instructing my son to take him back to Pete's body to go back over what had happened, a compassionate policeman stepped forward saying that was totally inappropriate. It is hard to believe someone could not foresee what long-term trauma could occur.

Once home, with the boy's safe, I felt I had to do something but had no idea what. I collected candles, gold and white organza flowers, and a simple green garland which hung on our front door every Christmas. Within minutes it was transformed into a beautiful little circular wreath with the candles standing upright in the midst of flowers. I felt compelled to go back to where Pete had been killed so I quietly left my stunned family and drove to the tiny one-way lane.

It was now dark and finding the spot where I sensed Pete had been killed I sat on the ground in the silent night. Lighting the candles, I took out the police reports and spoke to this man, whom I had only met once at my front door, about what a shock it must have been to have left so suddenly, and explained it was completely safe for him to go to the light.

At that moment the previously still night was interrupted by a powerful wind coming from nowhere. At the same time a large owl swooped down towards me with a single call. As instantly as both had arrived they were gone. The night returned to silence. Placing the candles and flower wreath on rock ledges at the side of the lane, I no longer felt the fear I arrived with, and left feeling exceptionally peaceful.

The next morning Pete's family friend was asked by his brothers to take them to the site. She told me later that, although she had been so afraid, as soon as she saw the candles and flowers, her fear disappeared. In that moment the place felt sacred. Although she had no idea who had done it, she felt so grateful someone had already been there and honoured Pete.

For all involved this experience was the beginning of a life-changing journey. Pete's death sent ripples through many families, the community and the tree industry, and resulted in long-term changes for everyone touched by this experience.

Tryphena McShane

Create your own wreath or garland to mark a sacred place.

Workplace accidents

It's easy to overlook workplace accidents especially as the majority of people directly affected by them are men, who often don't know how to deal with or speak of the horror these accidents bring. Often the most dangerous and dirty work is done by men. It's important we acknowledge and respect the very real risks many men take, and remember they have homes, personal aspirations, partners, siblings, pets, friends, parents and children.

Partners and families of those who die at work often find themselves overwhelmed at having to face the reality of their loved ones never coming home and needing to come to terms with the often deeply traumatic and un-expected way they died. One very brave woman explained how difficult it was for her to read the coroner's report of her husband's death. She knew she had to do so to make sense of what happened. Once she had read and processed it, she put it away somewhere safe where her children would not find this confronting information until they were adults when she would give them the option to read it.

For this woman the long-term ongoing counselling her family received made all the difference to her children. For herself, she knew she had to get on with life and keep her children protected. She was so caught up in dealing with the pain of her immediate family, for a long time she didn't see what was happening to extended family. 'I came a poor last for a long time,' she reflects. 'It was years before I got a look-in. By the time I got to it, I suppose it was somewhat easier for me as it was less raw. I had spent such a long time looking after my children, who each dealt with it in such different ways. Being aware of self-destructive tendencies and helping them work through the grief took all of my attention.

'I couldn't have got through this without the love and support of my brothers, sisters and their children. I have a wonderful close family. Sisters who were on the end of the phone in the middle of the night and dropped everything to drive to be with me when I needed help, and a network of amazing friends who even now constantly check up on me and include me in social and family activities. Once again, out of something so terrible I have discovered other things that are now very special to me.'

One of her children remembers how at the time when their counsellor had said, 'One day, a few years down the track, you will again be happy and able to feel the sunshine', she thought that impossible. But as time went by she found the counsellor was right.

Her brother-in-law, concerned with practical issues, said, 'I am eternally grateful that my brother had full insurance cover, so money problems weren't added to my sister-in-law's already devastating experience.'

It is often not only the fatality of a fellow worker or family member that causes intense hardship, but the ongoing stress at witnessing these events causing post-traumatic stress or survivor's guilt. War photographer Don McCullin says: 'People don't realise that smells, as well as vision, can be a very powerful memory. I don't care how strong a man thinks he is, eventually he will need an emotional arm around him.'

Aaron talks of a dream he had a few nights after Pete's death. He stepped up to take over Pete's workload. He did this by carrying Pete on his back everywhere he went, with Pete guiding him. They worked together happily. When asked if this frightened him Aaron said, 'No. It felt as though somehow Pete was telling me everything was okay. Nothing seemed strange in the dream at all. I had willingly agreed to become Pete's body for that moment to enable him to complete his work. Everything seemed in perfect order.'

Acknowledging someone who has been lost at work is essential—allowing close workmates to participate in the funeral and assist with the wake can help them as well as the family. Different workplaces have come up with inspiring ways to acknowledge those they have lost—some have held fundraisers for a charity close to the person's heart, others have an industry/company trophy named in the person's honour, and others maintain their presence through displaying a photo or memorial plaque in the workplace. Sometimes workmates may feel uncomfortable about intruding on the family, not realising how much families appreciate knowing their loved one isn't forgotten.

One friend who lost her husband at work was touched to be taken out to lunch every year on the anniversary of her husband's death, even though it was well over a decade before. An annual phone call on the anniversary, Christmas cards and other gestures can mean so much.

Losing my husband
to suicide

One morning, I awoke thinking of life and celebration. It was our first grandchild's first birthday. As owner–operators of a music store in a small country town, I was there every day to open the shop. I left home that morning in time to swing by my son's house to give our birthday baby a grandmotherly 'I'm glad you're alive' hug. We planned to have the cake, presents and photos that evening after everyone got home from work. That never happened. Sometime shortly after noon, the day disintegrated.

*

Clide and I emigrated to Australia from the US in 1988 with our teenage children. Since boyhood Clide had dreamt of owning a music store and so within days of settling into our new community, he set about making his dream a reality.

For many years Clide had been physically sick and then, emotionally. Some years after arriving in Australia he was severely burnt in a house fire. Extensive use of morphine, at that time, ultimately made him immune to most types of pain relief in the following years.

While living in Montana, he ran a propane equipment business. In those days the effects of climbing into big underground tanks to make repairs was unknown. However, in years to come, his severe fibromyalgia was often linked to the poisonous fumes there. Clide's accidents and illnesses were extensive. It left him predisposed to chronic illness and unbearable pain. Over time he was in a never-ending cycle of pain and depression.

Support from the medical community wasn't forthcoming as, over the years, the word amongst the doctors in our small town was that he was just after drugs. Many a night when he couldn't stand the pain any longer, we would end up in the emergency ward of the local hospital, but mostly to no avail. We were left waiting for hours, as staff were unwilling to call a doctor to administer pain relief. Sleep became more and more difficult for him, so he took to watching TV non-stop, sitting up in his recliner chair, dozing whenever he could. He was self-medicating with alcohol and marijuana.

I moved out a few weeks after the last of the children left home. I could no longer sleep for fear that he'd fall asleep in his chair with a lit cigarette, which had happened before.

*

At the time of his death, Clide was living alone in our family home. He had cut his hair the previous week. I knew this represented something significant. As a flower child he had never been into haircuts.

The night before he died, he had called me at about 10 p.m., which was rather late for him. We had a wonderful talk about the family. We discussed our grandson's birthday the next day and the new grandbaby who was on the way in just a few months. When I got off the phone, I thought to myself, 'That is the best he has sounded in a long time. Maybe something is changing.'

The next day when a friend came into the shop and took my hand, leading me to the room out the back, I knew what was coming, yet I still made him say it. 'What's wrong? Tell me. Just tell me,' I said.

'He's done it, darling. He's done it. Clide's dead. There are pill bottles everywhere.'

Even though it was way too late, I made him call an ambulance. Somehow we managed to close the shop. My son and I went to the house. Clide was still sitting in his recliner. The Native American medicine-band bracelet he had worn all our married life was on the table next to him. Through it was scrolled a letter to me. We sat on the floor at his feet and talked to him.

I thanked him for the life we had shared and for being the wonderful father he had been to the children. My son spoke words of love and gratitude to him too. Eventually the tears came. Moving into another room, I sobbed uncontrollably with my son standing by my side.

We had four children, aged between 20 and 26. Two boys lived in town. One son lived in another city and our daughter overseas. We went to my place to make the calls. With the shop closed, word travelled quickly through our small town. A couple of friends arrived to cook dinner and help me through those difficult first few hours. As they left later that night, another friend of Clide's arrived to stay with me.

Although dismayed that the coroner insisted on an autopsy, I didn't feel I could object since it was a suicide. After the autopsy, the results showed he did not have a high level of alcohol or drugs in his system, other than the sleeping pills. I was grateful for this. The fact that he made a conscious choice to end his life from a clear and sober perspective brought reassurance to the children and I that this was his choice.

Knowing that Clide wanted to be cremated I had intended to do this as soon as the autopsy was completed. Fortunately, someone had suggested I contact Zenith and she advised me to ask our two children who weren't here if they wanted to view the body. In my grief this would never have occurred to me. Her experience was that people who weren't given that choice often became angry or regretful later at not having had the chance to say goodbye. When I offered the children this option, they both said yes immediately. That put a whole new perspective on things.

In order to preserve the body till they got here, Clide was kept at a funeral home, and I decided on a small private open-casket service there. A more public, larger memorial service was planned for the following week.

I feel certain that anyone who has experienced the death of a loved one knows the first few days happen by grace. Friends came by and offered words of comfort. They brought food and insisted I eat. Phone calls were made to notify family and friends. The children returned home. Options were discussed. Arrangements made. Venues booked. A memorial service planned.

Our local community-radio blues presenter told me he would be dedicating his next show to Clide. On hanging up the phone I went to my stereo and checked the reception. Yes, it was coming in loud and clear. I made a note to record the program the following night.

I spent most of that day and the next looking through bookcases, closet shelves and dresser drawers, trying to find Clide's notebook of poetry. Although he hadn't written any poetry in recent years, the poems he wrote in the early 1980s were precious. Many years ago, I had typed them up and put them in a book, but now when I wanted it most I couldn't find it. Feeling it was important for his friends, and more importantly his children, to remember the poet who had lived inside that broken body, I desperately wanted his poetry read at the memorial service.

Initially, my reason for the poetry was a gentle distraction from my emotional pain. It was a means of focusing beyond the grief. Two days into the search however, this had turned to frustration then anger.

The night arrived in a haze of plans, and still no poetry to be found. Minutes before the blues show began, I turned the radio on to set up the tape recording. The reception was bad. I couldn't even listen to the show, let alone record it. My simmering anger came to full boil. Between exclamations and cursing, I discovered the receiver didn't even have a FM antenna on it. Why hadn't this happened yesterday when I tested it? Tears pouring down my cheeks, I rummaged through the chest of drawers next to the stereo looking for the FM antenna. Tossing things out of the drawers left, right and centre, suddenly I saw it. There at the bottom of the pile of wires and old tape recordings was Clide's notebook of poetry!

'I've found it!' I exclaimed in amazement. 'I've found Clide's poetry!'

Just then the radio reception cleared. The signal was crystal clear. No FM antenna was needed. I knew in that moment Clide had interfered with the radio reception, causing me to search for the antenna in the one place I could find his poetry. He was free at last.

The memorial service was held at the surf club. It was large enough to hold the community, and looked out on the Pacific Ocean. Arriving early we made sure the hall was swept, incense was burnt to create sacred space, and the stereo system and speakers were set up. The kids and I picked out specific songs that had meant something special to Clide. He was 'The Music Man' and music would tell the story of his life.

It was important to me to have his ashes at the memorial service. We placed them at the head of the hall in a wooden box, next to his guitar, along with the hat he was never seen without and his Native American bracelet on the box. All four of our children wanted to speak, which totally amazed me as I couldn't possibly have stood up and spoken.

Our daughter spoke first of how all her friends envied her for having such a 'cool' dad. Our son remembered sitting in his bedroom, picking and strumming one of his dad's guitars, when Clide came in and said, 'Son, if you are going to play the guitar, you better listen to this', then handed him a Jimi Hendrix tape.

Another son reminisced about how his dad continually tried to talk him out of wanting to play the drums, but in the end bought him a drum set. By this time, our third son was in tears and could not speak. Standing at the front with his brothers' and sister's arms around him, he cried on behalf of us all.

Friends also spoke, quoting Shakespeare, telling Clide the results of the American basketball play-off game that had taken place since he died, and sharing with Clide that the new Paul Simon album had been released. Someone even made me laugh, which I thought impossible.

At the end of the service people were invited to come up to write a short private message to Clide and put it in the sealed box next to Clide's guitar. These messages would be buried underneath a rosebush in my garden. Clide had always bought me red roses.

Following the service, our family and Clide's closest friend walked to the beach where we scattered a portion of his ashes. Taking some each, we went our separate ways to spread them in the water or in the air, to say our final goodbyes.

I recalled that a few months before his death Clide had casually asked me what I wanted done with my own ashes when I died. I told him I'd like some of them scattered in the bay and some taken back to Montana to the family cabin. He then said, 'That's what I would like too. Will you do that for me?' At the time this didn't seem that strange as he had always said he would die before me. Remembering this, I kept some of his ashes to scatter at Hellroaring Falls in Montana.

Over the weeks following Clide's death, issues came up that we hadn't dealt with during the initial grieving. My son and I both felt hurt, and even angry, that Clide chose to die on Izak's first birthday. Now, these two events would forever be on the same day. Eventually, I realised that he hadn't done that on purpose. Even though we had discussed Izak's birthday on the night that he prepared to take his own life, I don't think it actually occurred to him they would be on the same day.

He was ready to go. He had obviously planned it for months. He took approximately five months' worth of sleeping pills that night. This meant he had gone without sleeping pills for five months in preparation for that moment. The time had arrived. I don't think it occurred to him that any one day he died would be better or worse than another. This was just the day.

For the first few years, on that day it felt like we focused on Clide's death, and, oh yeah, it's Izak's birthday. After a couple of years, it became the day of Clide's death *and* Izak's birthday. A couple of years after that it became Izak's birthday *and* the day of Clide's death. And last year, it was just Izak's birthday. Although we all thought of Clide on that day, we didn't actually talk about it with each other. Not deliberately. It just happened that way.

Although the children and I were heartbroken about his death, there was also a great relief that he was no longer suffering. We were all exhausted from his suffering. We had all suffered with him because of our love for him. We had all watched him, sat with him, argued with him about what might give him some relief. The relief from the suffering did enable us to embrace his death as a blessing.

As the years roll on, one of the hardest things for us to accept is that the next generation will not get to know their big-hearted, generous, funny, music-loving grandfather. The fact that he wrote a clear coherent letter right before he died also comforted us. The letter was very typical of him. In spite of the sadness, even his sense of humour came through. The fact that he wasn't intoxicated at the time of his death also brought us great comfort and acceptance. For years we had shown him our love, encouraging him in dealing with the body he had. I don't think any of us experienced the guilt that families of suicides are often left with.

The significant gift for me of Clide's tragic death was learning how to live without the guilt associated with a loved one's suicide. At the age of eighteen, my brother had been diagnosed with schizophrenia. I cared for him for eleven years, until his suicide when he was 29. For the next thirteen years I suffered from untold guilt, before realising it had become a driving factor in my life. Undertaking a course of study and daily practice was what eventually dissolved that guilt. The next New Year's Eve, I made a promise to myself that I would live a guilt-free life from that moment on. Five days later Clide died from suicide.

I was given the gift of living my intention from new ground up. I now had the opportunity to live my commitment, not from a memory of a suicide but from the actual raw experience of a fresh suicide. I will always be grateful to Clide for teaching me so very much about life.

Gayle Cue

When someone takes their own life

Suicide is one of the hardest deaths to come to terms with. Should you be facing this sad situation, it's important to remember no-one is to blame. It's not unusual for those left behind to blame themselves, and to feel they have failed as a friend or loved one. To have avoided this is not always possible. However much you love someone, you may not be able to prevent them taking their own life.

Not surprisingly, suicide can provoke intense responses, from shock and confusion, to rage, guilt and blame. This too is normal. Diane tells of the pain and fear her family struggled with when they discovered her husband, and father of their two teenagers, had attempted suicide, and only survived because of the unexpected failure of both methods he used. Like many men, her husband suffered from the misguided belief that he must be strong, no matter what. 'Counselling and getting help for his very low self-esteem and toxic shame made such a difference,' Diane says.

Depression is often well hidden, particularly when it occurs in teenagers, or men. They may be afraid to talk about their feelings. It is only in hindsight that Diane now knows the warning signs: weight change, sleeplessness, putting himself down, becoming easily upset or being verbally aggressive, withdrawing, or wanting to pretend everything is normal. She also now understands that an upswing in mood for no apparent reason can also spell danger.

Sandra, who for 30 years struggled with drug and alcohol addiction after experiencing severe childhood abuse, joined a Suicide Anonymous twelve-step program. She says, 'I discovered children of a suicide parent can be more likely to think suicide is a solution. As I didn't want to be responsible for starting that in my family, I knew I needed all the help I could get, so I reached out and was amazed it really was there.'

Many people like Clide endure years of physical pain and emotional distress before making the decision to put an end to their suffering. Although this hurt his family, it helped that they were able to understand and accept his decision. By supporting each other and putting their energy into creating a personally meaningful ceremony, this helped them move through the confusion and pain.

Feelings of numbness and shock immediately after a suicide are normal. It is common for people to mindlessly continue on with daily lives while isolating themselves from others emotionally. Generally, friends want to be supportive but may not know what to do to help.

There are numerous ways you can help support people through the pain they are experiencing from the impact of suicide. Taking the time to open up a conversation and unconditionally listen to their experiences can be so healing for them. A young man whose teenage brother had committed suicide shared his relief that someone cared enough to broach the subject with him. He was grateful to be talking about it. Concerned that his own risk was highest after weekends, when the drugs and alcohol he tried to cover his pain with wore off, leaving him depressed, he was really glad to be having a conversation about suicide. He said so many people avoid discussing it, but that can feel very isolating. He was glad to know where it was safe for him to go to get support should he need it.

Helping someone to write about their loved one, in a poem or short story, focusing on the wonderful happy moments they shared, is another helpful way to spend time together. Writing down one's feelings can be very therapeutic.

Suicide.org has set up a section on its website called the 'Wall of Angels Suicide Memorials' where you can add the name of your own loved one, a photo and 'remembering an angel' information about them. This not-for-profit site is dedicated to suicide prevention, awareness and support, and can be found at www.suicide.org.

If posting memories of a loved one on a public website does not feel right, then a special, password-protected website can be created just for family and friends to access, which can be very healing, especially for those who are separated by distance.

The creation of a memorial garden, either in a private garden or, with the support of the local council, in a public park, can draw people of the community together to nurture a communal garden, and each other, and can also bring great solace. The garden may be full of flowers or mixed with vegetables to provide sustenance for those in need.

A woman, whose husband had taken his own life, talked to an artist friend about his love of frangipanis. Her artist friend asked her to collect flowers and leaves from a plant her husband had grown and to dry them. Mixing them with paint, the artist created a painting of four frangipani flowers, floating in a sky of stars, for her friend, who said, 'This painting is so comforting to me. Knowing it was painted with my whole family in mind, depicting each of us in such a heartfelt way, means so much to me. We have it in a special place in our home where I can look at it every night.'

My teenage son died on the road

They were supposed to go fishing and sleep on the island in the lake that night. For some reason my son Michael and his mates decided to go to a seventeenth birthday party instead. He had been at work all day and he, his brother Adam and three friends left home at about 5 p.m. As they left I called out, 'Be good.' Michael came back, laughingly saying, 'I can do what I like now I'm eighteen.' He had turned eighteen the week before.

*

'That was the night our family became intimately involved in Michael's story,' recalls Trypheyna. 'It was eleven on a Saturday night, a time of partying for most teenagers. We had been watching a movie when we heard the noise of young people laughing and talking at the top of our driveway on their way down the hill. Our son Aaron, who was sixteen at the time, had been grounded that weekend, so he was at home with us rather than at the party at the top of the hill, where his friends had gone. When he heard young people meeting near our house Aaron went out to see what was going on.'

'I went out because our letterbox had been smashed and stolen several times and I wanted to make sure this wouldn't happen again,' Aaron explains. 'When I got out the front, my dad joined me and I said to him, "It's my friends coming back from a party. They're not the ones who destroyed our letterbox." Heading up the drive to speak to them I heard the sound of a car coming down the road very fast. It was a red station wagon and as it screamed past our place it hit my friend Michael. I saw him cartwheel over the roof of the car and land on his head at the top of our neighbour's driveway.'

Aaron's dad Alex was on the porch waiting for the group of teenagers to continue walking down the hill, so he could go back inside to watch the movie. 'Hearing the sound of a vehicle, a powerful V8 engine in full roar, coming down the hill, I stopped to watch and listen,' Alex says. 'As the car passed on full throttle I heard an almighty thud when it reached the group of kids, then it continued down the hill. I was very aware of the fact that the engine tone and speed had not changed at all, and that I had just witnessed a hit-and-run. Running up the drive I looked around for what the vehicle had hit.

'It took several moments to realise there was someone lying in a heap on the road. Immediately I ran to the person and saw that he was unconscious, lying with limbs in an unnatural position. I noticed blood trickling from his right ear and that the pupils of his eyes were fully dilated. This seriously injured teenager was breathing with long jagged breaths spaced far apart.

'I chose not to move him, due to the severity of his injuries. I was very aware of gritting my teeth, suppressing my emotions and choosing to go into a very cold, focused, logical and efficient mode of operating.'

Trypheyna, who was in the house with their youngest daughter when the accident happened, recalls: 'When I heard the sound I jumped up, knowing that I had to go out there to see what I could do to help, but absolutely terrified of what

I would see. I struggled to drag my brain out of its stunned, fearful state, forcing it into logical thought. What would be needed up there?

'While I raced to get blankets and pillows Aaron called the ambulance. All he could tell me was that someone had been hit and the car had kept going.'

'When we got up there my friends on the road and sidewalk were hysterical, drunk and very scared,' Aaron says. 'Although I felt shocked this was happening to my mates, right outside my home, on a night when I should have been out there partying with them, I didn't have time to focus on that. I just knew I had to take control of the situation and calm people down. I needed to make sure Michael had enough space around him and wouldn't be affected by their screaming.

'His younger brother, Adam, who had also been grazed by the car, was eerily calm. I think he was probably in shock. I took him and the others to the side of the road to sit and wait for the ambulance to arrive, leaving Mum to look after Michael and Alex to deal with the traffic that was still trying to drive down the road.'

Trypheyna says, 'It was a terrifying cacophony of sound, a mass of screams. Whatever state the young man was in, he did not need to be in the middle of this panic-stricken howling and mayhem. I was so grateful Aaron knew instantly to calm the kids down and to get them to stop screaming.

'He was lying on a steep section of the hill, face up, with his head lower than his feet. After gently placing blankets over his body, I sat down on the road next to him. Feeling quite helpless, I did the only thing I knew; I gave him reiki, a form of "hands on healing", channelling loving energy through my hands. I talked to him, telling him he was safe, and that the ambulance was on its way. I knew he was unconscious but I understood the importance of communicating lovingly with people even if they appear to be in a coma. On some level I felt he knew I was there.

'That night something precious happened. Even today I can still reach into that place and draw on those timeless moments spent with Michael.'

*

At about 1 a.m., I was dozing on the sofa when Adam came screaming into the house: 'Mum! Michael's been hit!' I thought he meant punched. 'No, the car didn't stop!' That's when I realised a car had hit him. Adam was distraught, ranting and raving about others also being hit, and that he'd been hit as well. I asked, 'Where are they?' and he said they'd been taken to the hospital.

I woke my husband. We have a large family and, unable to take all our other kids with us, I grabbed our three year old and we took off to our local hospital, assuming this was where they had taken Michael. When we arrived we learnt one of the other boys who'd been hit was there, but Michael had been taken to a larger hospital. I asked to see the other boy. His arm was injured and I told the nurses to get in touch with his parents straightaway.

It was so chaotic trying to organise family and friends to take care of the younger children so we could get to the hospital. Adam was there in the background, but in deep shock. We didn't have the time to support him in the way he needed because all our focus was on getting to be with Michael. On the drive there I kept telling Adam everything would be alright but I had a dreadfully uneasy feeling. I felt really cold even though it was a lovely warm night. It was very clear, with a full moon.

At the hospital there were three people waiting to greet us, including a social worker. I knew it had to be bad, really bad. We kept saying we wanted to see Michael but he had been taken away for scans. We insisted on seeing him as soon as he was back. I remember looking at Adam and seeing his tears. He was shaking, absolutely shaking. It was so distressing.

We were told Michael was brain dead and the machine was breathing for him. That was it. They didn't give us any hope. There wasn't any hope. They told us they would have to bring in another neurosurgeon to do the same CAT scans again to support the diagnosis. In all, three specialists examined him but the outcome was the same.

It was suggested we go home and talk to the rest of our family then bring them all to the hospital to say goodbye to Michael. We were in such a daze, doing everything on automatic. Michael's boss turned up. I had no idea how he heard about it but I was touched to know Michael mattered that much. We stayed at the hospital all day and the following night.

They asked us about organ donation. As a family we discussed it. Some of us agreed but others were not too happy, so we decided we would donate only some of his organs. We decided not to give away Michael's heart, and for some reason my eldest son said not his lungs. I definitely didn't want to give away his eyes because I had always loved his beautiful shining eyes.

We now believe that if we'd been told there would be an autopsy and been fully informed of what that involved, we would have made very different choices and donated everything, including his heart and lungs.

Later on we learnt they had been totally wasted. They were cut up during the autopsy. We will never really be sure what was put back into his body. We know his brain wasn't. In the end parts of him were disposed of as human garbage. By the time we found out it was too late. It is awful to think we made our decision for sentimental reasons when there is such a long waiting list for heart and lungs.

After saying goodbye to Michael, my family was determined to find the vehicle that had hit him and the person driving it, as the police had been unable to come up with anything. They had no leads. Family and friends set off to search every street in the neighbourhood. They found the car, tucked away in some bushes near a church, with all its damage including a broken headlight.

After finding the car it was only a short step to discovering who owned it and who had been driving it that night. The police arrested a nineteen year old. He'd been at the same party as Michael, drinking heavily and smoking marijuana. Tragically for us he decided to drive home that night heavily intoxicated.

I have been told that as he left the party, other teenagers, who recognised he shouldn't be driving, tried unsuccessfully to persuade him to take a bike or skateboard to get home instead. If only those teenagers had felt safe to speak to a responsible adult that night, it might have changed the whole course of events.

I don't believe in God but I've come to believe in destiny. I now believe Michael's death was destiny. He had already safely passed that dangerous spot on the road but went back up in defence of a friend who was being harassed. He was reaching out to defend someone he thought was at risk.

For myself, I have now found a reason to survive. Everyone has to have a reason to go on.

At first I felt like I had no control. Then I looked at the bigger picture. I now actively lobby politicians to change laws to support families who have become victims of similar experiences. I learnt how to research, and refuse to be put off by doors closing in my face. People might say I have become harder these days, but I won't accept anything less than the truth anymore. I discovered I could affect my world far more than I ever believed possible. The main thing I've learnt from this is to listen to my instincts. I think deep down we sometimes let our brains think for us when we should be going with our feelings. As a result of Michael's death I am much stronger than I used to be.

*

When considering the aftermath, Trypheyna writes: We can't afford to lose our young people like this. The impact is massive. This hit-and-run was the direct result of the deadly combination of drink, drugs and dangerous driving which not only ended the life of a young man but almost split a community apart. Additionally, earlier requests to the local council to make the road safer had continually fallen on deaf ears and the lack of a footpath, long identified by residents as 'an accident waiting to happen', made this death all the more tragically unnecessary. After Michael's death, determined insistence from concerned citizens resulted in council finally undertaking the much-needed roadworks to make the road safe for school children and other pedestrians.

Chris Green and friends

Unexpected outcomes

Death can have many different and surprising outcomes resulting from what people are faced with, and choose to do, after a death. Deaths caused by unnecessary accidents or someone's deliberate intent to harm can add a whole new dimension to the already tragic experience of losing a loved one. It's difficult enough to come to terms with the fact that someone we love has died unexpectedly, without having to deal with these additional factors.

When such events transpire, ripples of angst and disbelief can also cause divisiveness within communities and between individuals. Grief-stricken victims of crime may attempt to take justice into their own hands to avenge the person who has died. After Michael's death, caused by a hit-and-run driver, his friends were frustrated at the lack of justice and wanted to do something about it themselves. While understandable, this can cause even deeper grief for the family, because attention is forced away from their natural grieving process and they feel responsible for mediating a solution between warring factions. Michael's mother, Chris, spent a lot of time supporting his grieving teenage friends. She explained that more violence would serve no purpose and that, instead, Michael's death needed to be honoured. This shows how important it is for a community to be able to find ways to release hostility which, if left, would explode, compounding the tragedy.

These terrible situations can inspire wonderful solutions. Those not immediately impacted by the death can help gather friends together, giving them the opportunity to express and release their grief, rage, sorrow and fear, by encouraging them to connect with each other.

Chris says, 'I have always known that the body can endure a great deal of pain, but mental pain is far worse. It amazed me how much mental pain we are capable of bearing. If you break a leg, the body recovers over time, pain is no longer a constant companion. By contrast, mental pain fills up your mind constantly. It's vital to change that; something good has to come out of it. You have to find a way to transmute it.'

By channelling this pain it can become a force for change— such as the choice to build a skate park, create some community art, plant a memorial garden, make dedication CDs and movies, hold a fundraising dance or write letters to bring about community change.

Many unexpected things have come from intense grief. Laws have been changed, funding made available, community support systems created, submissions made to parliament, dangerous environments fixed, medical equipment purchased, and many other important changes have resulted from the death of a loved one. Michael's tragic death brought about a new initiative called the 'Out of Harm's Way' agreement (www.warringah.nsw.gov.au/outofharmsway). This one-page contract is lovingly dedicated to Michael, who taught a community how important it can be to take those extra steps in order to help keep each other safe. It is designed to initiate discussion on drug and alcohol use, personal safety, looking after friends and getting home safely. The contract is aimed at getting families to communicate, so parents and teenagers can make an agreement together.

Chris Green explains the process: 'Adults agree to be available for help at any time, day or night, to respond without anger, and to talk over any details calmly at another time. The young person agrees never to drive while intoxicated, or get in a car with someone who is, and to seek help for themselves and their friends, regardless of the time or situation. Many parents assume their teenagers already know they are always there to help, no matter what. However, because they are often doing things their parents might disapprove of, many young people feel that they couldn't possibly call on them, even in an emergency.

'You can easily draft an agreement of your own and that single piece of paper might one day save a life.'

Ken Marslew began 'Enough is Enough' after his son was murdered in a senseless robbery at Pizza Hut, as he tried to come to terms with his terrible grief. Ken discovered what a difference it made to bring together the victim's family and the perpetrator with appropriate support people so everyone could hear each other's stories. The power of hearing the other person's story can never be underestimated. When you don't know the full story, it is easy to invent scenarios, motivations and circumstances, and these assumptions can cause additional unnecessary pain. Research shows that once a perpetrator understands the impact of their actions on so many people, their rate of re-offending drops dramatically. Remarkably, Ken now mentors the young man who killed his son in panic when the robbery went wrong.

Chris Green has helped make changes to the law and says: 'It is so important to find your own voice because it can feel as though everything else has been taken away from you. Put yourself in the most uncomfortable position and take your power back. Open doors, change the big picture, fight for justice. I always ask people, "Are you getting the answers you need?" I've found a need to know everything. Some people think they will protect you by not giving you answers, not realising this can cause extra pain. I discovered from talking to others in the same position that almost everyone felt they needed to know everything. There are legal avenues available to help make sense of what occurred; for example, you have the right to ask the coroner's court to undertake an enquiry.'

Sometimes victims of crime or accidents also have to deal with media attention. Should you find yourself in the media spotlight, as Tony and Angela did after their daughter Anna died after taking ecstasy, it might be wise to follow their advice: 'Make the media your friends.' They wanted to make sure other teenagers weren't put in Anna's position. By embracing the media in a low-key dignified way, they found themselves supported caringly in the telling of their story.

When dealing with the media you do need to be savvy. It's not advisable to just tell your story and hope that the reporters will do a good job for you. It's far too easy for your words to become unintentionally slanted and cause you unnecessary pain. If you choose to allow the media to write your story, then it is advisable to give permission only after you have seen what's been written. You can also write your own account. If they really want your story, and you are clear they are to use your words or nothing, your story will be told fairly. Protect yourself and your loved ones, and follow your instincts.

Finally, Chris Green has some powerful advice on the importance of personal responsibility and growth: 'To the person who has created the chaos, I say, "Don't waste your second chance. You have a second chance, your victim doesn't, so take responsibility. I admire someone who says, *I am responsible and I am so sorry. I've robbed your family of birthdays and weddings for the rest of your lives.* Take ownership, it will help lift the burden off the innocent people who otherwise end up having to carry it."'

Come together with loved ones in remembrance.

Losing our daughter
to ecstasy

People die every day, but this one event changed everything for us: the shape, the colour, the form of everything. We became totally different people.

When our eldest daughter Alice was born I had an epiphany. This tiny baby changed my life from being an independent young woman. I had to ask, 'What on earth have I been doing with my life till now?'

The same thing happened with Anna's death. The life-changing force was equal. After Anna died nothing was ever the same again. Nothing. She was only fifteen when she died after taking an ecstasy tablet with her friends at a club. This was a time when many parents knew little about the recreational drugs young people were taking. It was Sunday morning. I hadn't slept that night. Our stepdaughter and family had been over for dinner. We had a great night with a couple of glasses of wine, but I couldn't sleep. I went down-stairs to get Saturday's papers and read them from cover to cover, watching the clock.

I didn't know it then, but Anna was in the house across the street, less than a hundred yards away. At 8 a.m. I went to bed, and less than half an hour later was woken by a banging on the door.

'Anna's sick! Anna's sick!'

I pulled something on and ran over.

She was still dressed, lying on a bed in an upstairs bedroom. 'What have you done to my daughter?' I demanded. I picked her up and said, 'Come on Anna, it's Mum.' I got her upright, but she collapsed in my arms and didn't recognise me. She must have had a terrible headache as she had a huge bruise on her head.

After bringing her back, extremely unwell, from the club in the city, her friends were too afraid to let any adult know where they had been or what they had been doing. They had put her in the room to sleep and shut the door. During the night she must have got up, staggered to the door and collapsed, hitting her head.

I struggled to carry her then Tony arrived and we got her down the stairs. Tony was saying, 'Don't die. Please don't die.' At that moment she stopped breathing. Tony knew Anna had died in his arms.

The ambulance seemed to take forever to get there. On arrival they immediately put her on oxygen and on hearing she had been in the city gave her Narcan, thinking she had overdosed. They resuscitated her. I was angry because they kept asking so many questions about drugs and I kept thinking, 'But she's only a little girl for goodness sake! What do drugs have to do with this?'

We followed the ambulance to hospital and ran into the emergency ward. We were met by a young doctor, a beautiful-looking man in his late 20s, who immediately took Anna into an emergency room. We were asked to sit in a small ante-room that I referred to as 'the death room'. I felt so helpless waiting there, so I went outside to a wet, grey, misty morning and stood in a nearby graveyard. Walking in the rain I wanted to scream at God, 'Why?' At that moment I knew she had gone. I felt so angry.

As I re-entered the hospital my phone rang. It was one of Anna's friends telling me, 'Mrs Wood, I know what Anna has done. She has taken ecstasy.'

I said, 'What's ecstasy?'

How does a sixteen year old tell you what ecstasy is? They didn't take it to die. They took it to have fun. How could they possibly have explained it to me? I had no idea but I was soon to find out.

I went back into 'the death room' to join Alice, Tony and Julie, our exchange student. We sat together silently. Suddenly I looked up to my right and saw my deceased father. His beautiful smiling face was looking down at me. I asked Alice if she could see him too. She could. I turned to Tony and said, 'I can see Dad, can you see him?'

He said, 'No, but I can see my own father and he is smiling at me.'

We both knew then that they had come for Anna. 'We'll look after her, don't worry,' their smiles were telling us. It meant so much.

The young doctor came in with tears in his eyes and said, 'I'm so sorry. I can't save her. I can't save your daughter. She has brain damage.'

I thought, 'You poor thing, a 40-hour shift on a Saturday night. I'm not listening to you because I know you're exhausted.' Even though our fathers had appeared to us, part of me wasn't going to give up. Anyone who has lost a loved one knows you don't think logically at a time like that.

While we were waiting and talking about her, we were surprised to discover that none of us had ever felt Anna was destined to grow old. Later I came across an entry in her diary which said, 'I know I am only fifteen but I have a feeling my time on this earth is short, so I suppose I should make the most of it!' She died the following month.

In conversation over dinner Anna had once told us she wanted to donate her organs. The hospital struggled with this because although she was clinically dead, her body was being kept alive on machines and they didn't want to appear interested only in her organs.

Tony reassured them that was what Anna wanted. He says, 'Anna was a giver. She gave right up to the end, even her organs. The strangest thing was that every one of her organs was working perfectly, the only one damaged was her brain. Later, we had at least five cards from people who were so grateful to have them. I have come to understand that they were in fact only spare parts. The spirit is the most important thing and Anna is still around.'

It was a large funeral with more than 600 people and full TV coverage. Many newspapers carried an article on the death of Anna Wood. So many people were touched by her death. Anna suddenly became everybody's daughter. We cooperated with the media because we were anxious to avoid this happening to other young people. We wanted teenagers to know how important it is to get help when in trouble.

In the week after Anna's death, I had a powerful dream. I was in a railway-station waiting room in a big coat, looking down the platform waiting for a steam train. Through a door came Anna, looking as though she was going to school, in a mixture of uniforms, partly primary, partly high school. Two other girls I recognised were sitting there. She came into my arms. It was such a wonderful sensation. I held her. I smelt her skin, my nose in her neck. It was so beautiful. I wanted it to go on forever. We hugged for a long time. I felt so peaceful. She kept saying, 'I'm really, really happy Mum.' I could see it. Then, beaming, she said, 'Mummy—I've got to go. I have so much to do. I can't stay.'

One of girls in the waiting room said, 'Anna, you're real.'

The other girl said, 'No she's not, she's dead.'

Taking Anna's left hand, the first girl reached out to her, saying, 'No! That's not true! Feel her!'

The second girl then said, 'Oh my God, I can feel it.'

In my dream, I said to Anna, 'Promise you'll come and see me again, darling.'

'You will see me again, but not for a long, long time,' she said, then dropped my hand and walked out the door. I could still smell her. She always smelt so good.

I woke Tony, saying, 'I've just been with Anna, she's really well and happy.'

He smiled, adding, 'Next time you see her, will you ask her to come and see me, as I need to see her.'

During this intense time, Tony and I received a personal letter from an editor at HarperCollins publishers saying that as a mother she could feel our pain. She talked of her concern for other teenagers and how she thought there was a vital book to be written. This was the birth of *Anna's Story*, written by Bronwyn Donaghy. It was published and available for school students only three months after Anna died, an extraordinary feat. Clearly this story needed to be told.

There wouldn't have been many parents in the country who didn't recognise Anna's face. The book had an enormous impact. I think her beautiful face intrigued everyone. They could all identify with her. She was so full of the promise of youth.

After the book came out we were asked to speak in schools all over the country. Talking about Anna was food for my soul. Girls would usually want to come up and touch me. If a boy hung around I knew I needed to talk to him. One day three boys waited for me. One asked, 'Would you mind if I painted Anna?' His exquisite painting now welcomes everyone into our home. Other school friends, in the band Schneider's Ape, produced a very professional song which included Anna's diary entries written to her imaginary friend Shefa.

After several years of speaking in schools and colleges, we felt burnt out and returned to England, hoping for a complete change of lifestyle. We ran a pub in the Lake District, opposite a secondary school which hosted summer programs. One of the delegates, a French translator of books and documents, came into the pub and got chatting with Tony. They talked about their girls and when he shared that his daughter had leukaemia, Tony gave him *Anna's Story*. Within 24 hours he had read the book and returned to tell us it had to be translated and published in France. Committed to reaching as many teenagers as possible, we agreed. Before long it was translated by Brid Kehoe, titled '*Anna au Pays des Merveilles*': *L'Ecstasy meurtrière* (Anna in Wonderland: Killer ecstacy), and was on the shelves of French bookshops and schools.

This was obviously another challenge Anna had set for us. There were then three trips to France, talking to teenagers with the aid of a translator. On the third visit I suffered a fall, fractured a neck vertebra and broke both wrists. In my healing process, these challenges have taught me to take time out to look after myself. You cannot rush healing. My true healing had begun.

I believe Anna was bringing me home. Though it is not my birthplace, somehow I feel more secure in Australia. Anna had constantly told me: 'Open your eyes. Don't just look. See. Don't just hear. Listen.' Hanging on my wall is a photo I took of Anna that I love. She is sitting on the floor, talking on the phone, and there is a single gum leaf lying in front of her. Now, if she wants to get in touch, she leaves me a leaf. It was strange that even in England, where those trees don't grow, gum leaves would appear. The gift Anna has given me is much greater understanding. I know I now have enough knowledge to see the light in everything.

*

I'd been an atheist for a long time. I went to a strict Catholic boys' school and often got the strap. I was dyslexic and had ADHD, which no-one understood back then. It was at this time I rejected God, the church and the spirit world all at once.

When Anna was young, my wife Angela and I ran a pub in England. Anna became close friends with a family who visited regularly. After she died they called us unexpectedly in

Australia. These were not the type of people to make a call like this. They told us: 'When we left the pub on Sunday evening, Anna was there waiting. She said, "Tell my dad I'm very sorry about what happened but I'm really happy." She said to tell you she didn't ever mean to hurt you.'

The family said they knew they had to call, because every morning when backing the car out of their house to take their son to school, Anna had been sitting on the fence post. She said she wouldn't go away until they rang me. This was a very confronting experience for them. I was still raw and hurting. Even though they had given me this information, the pain was terrible. There is nothing as painful as losing your child. For a long time I was consumed by anger. There was a vice around my heart. I felt as though I couldn't breathe. The anger kept me alive; I might have hurt myself otherwise.

Strange things began to happen. We would talk about Anna and lights would dim, almost go out, and then come back on again. Alice had always been much more open to everything than I ever was, and she saw Anna a lot after she died. About a year after Anna's death, I was with my brother on a boat when she came to me. We had a 'mental' conversation. She said, 'I am so sorry. I didn't mean to hurt you. I'm really fine helping the young ones who die and are confused when they arrive.' Then she said something strange, 'They don't call me Anna, they call me Cathy Broadarms.' Fading away she said, 'I'll see you again.' She's never been back. She did what she could to relieve my pain and moved on.

As a result of that experience my faith returned, and I was able to forgive the kids who were with Anna the night she died and the girl who gave her the ecstasy. I also forgave myself. Anna was always my mate—she was more fun than a barrel of monkeys, so cheeky it was hard to rouse on her. We couldn't have done anything different. Somehow I believe that what happened to Anna was meant to happen. We couldn't have loved her more, nor known the extraordinary gifts she would leave for each of us.

Our elder daughter Alice blew her top on one occasion when a TV interviewer asked her what issues were the underlying reasons why Anna had taken drugs. 'Because they're fashionable and available. I'm really lucky. My sister probably saved my life. For the end of high school I was going to take ecstasy to celebrate. I started my final exams the day after her funeral. It could well have been me.'

Anna touched so many people through her death. Her gifts have been to remind parents to take greater care of their young, tell them how much they love them and encourage teenagers to reassess the belief that they are invincible. Ultimately, Anna showed us that this journey has not been about drugs. It has been about travelling to find the infinite within ourselves.

Angela and Tony Wood

Supporting teenagers

Death can visit our teenagers from many unexpected directions through the death of parents, grandparents, brothers and sisters, wider family and friends. In teen years friends are especially important as are friends' families, teachers, mentors and, should they have a job, workmates.

Transitioning from childhood to adulthood they are already dealing with rampant hormones, new thought patterns and intense growth. Add death into this mix, and it can be a totally overwhelming experience. If the death of a loved one was violent or accidental, the result can be complete numbness. As growing teenagers are in the process of separating from their parents and lack adult resources for dealing with life, they may well be at greatest risk in dealing with death. Having to face the impermanence and vulnerability of life, along with their rage, fear, confusion, distress and despair, can be absolutely devastating.

Trypheyna recalls her teen daughter's experience: 'I remember my daughter's turmoil and disbelief when a teacher, who helped her deal with bullying, unexpectedly dropped dead from a heart attack. The whole school was in mourning for this charismatic man, needing help to come to terms with his death. I was so grateful that another teacher, realising my daughter was adrift and very vulnerable, stepped in to take over the support role for her. A year later, this healthy teacher also dropped dead of a heart attack on the school sportsfield. My daughter's distress was palpable.

'How do you explain this? I couldn't. All I could do was love her, take her to counselling and support her to find another champion teacher, which fortunately she was able to do. Death was teaching her some exceedingly powerful lessons. Each time she was knocked down she would have to get back up again, slightly stronger, but it took outside support for her to see this gift.'

Whatever the death, it's important teenagers know the truth. Share your own first experience of death. Help them to see that adults can help and do understand, as we all go through the same experiences. Encourage them to talk and, if appropriate, take part in preparations for the funeral.

Sometimes there's so much going on in life that you mightn't realise how much your teenager is hurting. They may not want to bother you with their grief, or may want to be 'adult' about it. Find ways to encourage them to tell you what help they want and what they feel will sustain them. They need to know everyone hurts. Often teenagers feel that only their peers under-stand or listen to them without judgement, and so cling to their friends at a time like this.

It's important teenagers know that there's nothing so bad they can't talk about it. Being loyal to their friends above any-thing else can have disastrous outcomes as they don't have the life skills to find the best solutions. They should be encouraged to tell the truth to adults who can help, and counselled that talking to adults does not mean disloyalty to friends. Letting someone know things are going wrong, or that friends are in trouble, can save lives and years of heartache for others. Early intervention could avert devastating results.

Most teenagers explore life and what it means to be an adult in the company of peers, and death is no exception. In their shock and disbelief they prefer to gather together, often finding solace in another teenager who has experienced a similar loss. They may do this by email or blogging with strangers. Sometimes the advice they get is good. Often it is not. It's important that adults stay close to them at this time—especially if there has been a suicide, as teen 'copycat suicides' can be a result. If they don't want to reveal their feelings to their parents, encourage them to talk freely to a close adult friend, or have that adult friend make the contact.

Girls and boys deal with death differently. Girls will generally talk and cry more easily, and this can encourage boys to feel and express their emotions as well. In the past young men in their late teens would traditionally have had a rite of passage, where they had to pass a series of physical tests. Now they often turn to alcohol and drugs, sex or acts of bravado as a form of release. These avenues make them vulnerable

Some teens may be unable to focus at school. Other grieving teenagers may prefer to have no disruption to their routine. Some may be open to counselling, while others may be completely opposed to the idea. Even if they don't want counselling, it could help parents to seek guidance, so that they know how best to support their sons or daughters.

Teenage suicide is more complex. For teens, who are often struggling with self-esteem, the complexities of growing up can feel like an impossible task sometimes. Then to see an outpouring of adoration from peers for their dead friend isn't necessarily helpful. They need to understand that it serves no purpose to follow suit as there's a lot of living yet to do. Teens are often not aware enough of the devastation they'd cause by choosing the same course of action. Research has shown that teens often have the misguided sense that they can take their own life and still be around to experience how people are affected by it afterwards. Although this makes no sense, it shows how heightened emotional intensity can sometimes override logical thought. It's helpful for parents to know pain and sadness are often accompanied by emotions such as confusion, guilt, emptiness and anger. These are absolutely natural and essential on the journey to acceptance.

At the funeral of a fourteen year old who had taken his own life, Zenith suggested:

Spend time together, share your pain and thoughts and help each other to get through this experience. It may take you a year or even longer to make any sense of things. Try not to get stuck in this moment, send his spirit off into the light, so it can fly free. Look for him in the night sky, in the waves of the ocean, and in the forest. Let him be at one with the elements from which we all come, and to which we all return.

When friends of mine die, we use a Buddhist practice that helps us with grief in the following weeks. We light candles to help their spirit on its journey. Each week for seven weeks we relight the candles on the day they died, enabling us to focus on them and to share how we feel as time passes. Gradually the pain becomes easier. Organise a time with your friends, wherever you are, to light candles and send love for ten minutes. Your collective energy will connect you all together.

Two babies, one heartbeat

When I was nineteen, I watched the documentary *Some Babies Die*, a moving exploration of the death of a baby. It was so profound, so intimate, tears ran down my cheeks in a constant stream. Not out of sadness alone, but also tears of joy, because death was not feared here. It was acknowledged, explored and blessed. The family truly experienced and celebrated life and death. Watching this, I felt a distinct shift inside and I knew this hour of TV would have a profound effect on the rest of my life.

My first marriage welcomed three gorgeous boys. My current partner, Adam, was hesitant to start a family early in our relationship, as we had four children between us from our previous relationships. I agreed in theory but then found I was already pregnant with twins. Termination was not an option.

I fiercely defended my unborn babies, realising that my newfound independence would enable me to do and be whatever I put my mind to. Single-parenting was not such a bad option. I turned all my energy to nurturing our unborn babies. I anticipated the future joys of our twins, feeling deep down that Adam would understand my commitment.

One night I had a dream in which my twins spoke to me. My little girl, who I had already named Indigo, told me she was coming just to visit and that she would always be with us, but in spirit only. Her brother Eli would represent her. She told me not to be sad, as this was the way things were meant to be.

I buried this dream, believing that pregnant women are often notoriously irrational, and that dreams are just a release of fears and emotions. Yet no matter how hard I tried to 'outsmart' or 'out-manoeuvre' this dark undercurrent, I still carried an uncomfortable feeling of impending doom. As my babies grew, so did my concern.

I resolved to eliminate all the known risks that could be encountered on my birth journey. I engaged two midwives. I read every prenatal book I could find and attended support groups, doctors' appointments, yoga and counselling. I was not willing to let my daughter die. My dream was not going to sabotage my life.

Curiously though, as time moved on, so did my attitude. I started to see life more spiritually. I felt I had put all these safety nets in place, truly done everything I could possibly do to prevent Indigo from dying, but deep down in my soul I realised that it was not in my power to change that. Somehow I had been forewarned of what was to come and, acknowledging this information as a gift, it gave me time to come to terms with it before the actual event.

The night before my labour began, the most primal force I have ever experienced gripped me. I wailed like a lone wolf, my body convulsing into sobs of raw emotion. I had no control over it. I realise now that this was when Indigo chose to leave. I sang her adieu.

The next morning, labour began normally. My midwives initiated foetal monitor checks. There was only one heartbeat. They told me the monitor's batteries were dead and they would need to be replaced, but I knew the truth. New batteries, same outcome.

Like a shroud, a different energy pervaded the birth space. Death. Indigo was stillborn. The vacuum of silence seemed fathomless, pierced only by Adam's heartbreaking sobs as he held our firstborn daughter. She was so beautiful, serene and perfect in every way, but I was in a surreal and alternate universe as it was imperative to birth Eli as soon as possible. A few minutes later, a healthy and very alive angelic boy whooshed into the water and lay on my breast alongside his sister Indigo.

Reverence pervaded the room. I had an overwhelming sense of gratitude that Eli was breathing and alive, while simultaneously humbled by Indigo's presence, her tangible essence. It was such an intense timeless moment that words can't fully express the torrent of emotions experienced.

After consultation we had decided to keep Indigo's body at home with us in a cooling unit for the next week. We especially wanted the children to experience their sister as much as they could. At the end of the week our families arrived and we created and held our own special ceremony at home. Spending this time together as a family and sharing our sadness allowed us to move forward together towards a gentle healing.

Zenith asked the crematorium if we could take Indigo there in a basket, rather than a traditional coffin, as we all felt this was less confronting. They agreed. So, after the ceremony, Adam took Indigo's body, resting on a pillow, in a small wicker basket. She was covered with flowers.

*

Now twelve years later, I feel so privileged to have been able to experience death in such a positive, life-affirming way. A year after Indigo's birth, amazingly we welcomed another set of twins, a girl and a boy. Indigo was the catalyst for deep growth and learning for our family. Her death strengthened our relationship. There are no regrets, no 'What if's', no 'If only's', just a simple truth—Indigo is dead but our daughter is not *just* a memory. She is our firstborn daughter, a loved, acknowledged member of our family. She shines every minute of every day in the sun and the stars, in the very air we breathe. She has changed our lives and perceptions forever, and I am eternally grateful for this.

Jodi Osborne

Death of little ones

You don't have to be a parent to imagine the pain and grief of losing a child. It's a parent's worst fear.

The death of a baby—whether in utero, at birth or shortly afterwards—is a devastating loss, particularly when everything is geared towards new life which instead turns into an unexpected death. What makes this loss harder is that labour has often been long and intense. The parents are already exhausted, then find themselves confronted by this heartbreaking loss.

In such cases it is important that parents are given as long as they need to fully experience their baby. This may involve taking baby home, bathing him, holding her, cuddling and nurturing their little one. A wonderful thing to do is take photographs and handprints or footprints, so these mementos can be long-term reminders of their beloved baby.

When Rosie and Bob, who were in their early 40s, lost their first child, it was a tragic experience for them as they were sure they were too old to have any more children. They decided to bury their little girl at sea, sending their dreams off with her. A friend gave them a beautiful old wooden box where they could store all their precious mementos of their baby. Some time later, the couple bumped into that friend and told her they did have another child. The box she had given them is now held in trust for their son, so he can know all there is of his sister.

The loss of a little one at any age is tragic. Parents need the full support of family, friends and community to help them through. Some parents are able to open their hearts and home to everyone, so that all may share their grief and loss. This is especially important for school-age children, as this may be the first experience of death for the friends left behind.

Holding the funeral ceremony in nature can feel less constricted and intense, and allows children to sit together on the ground or move around more freely. During a lengthy ceremony children often get up and wander, finding their own level of comfort.

For many children and adults this will be the first time they have seen a dead child. Children are naturally curious and, given the chance, will come and look in a small open coffin. They will ask simple questions and chat among themselves in the way children do. If adults try to answer their questions in an open and honest way, it helps children understand and accept death as a natural part of their lives, no matter what their level of development. By creating an appropriate, beautiful ceremony which celebrates a life, even the short life of a baby or child, family and friends may begin to come to terms with their loss.

Each parent deals with their experience differently. Family and friends are often so shocked they literally don't have the words. Simply acknowledging that this is a momentous time and that you are there for them can help enormously. Gently inviting them to show you their photos or other mementos can create an opening for parents paralysed by grief. Simple kindness, making meals, grocery shopping and being available to run errands can make all the difference.

Deep pain, sadness and grief is something they may or may not be able to work through, separately or together. Some relationships don't survive. Grief counsellors can be invaluable in helping bereaved parents work through the issues of guilt and blame, as these are often the areas that can create a huge gulf between a couple. It's also very important that parents are aware of not getting so lost in their grief that their other children or their partner suffer, feeling totally neglected. Honest and open communication is essential if parents are to maintain their relationship. This sort of grief can last for years.

Years after the death of a child, some parents say they feel they have become more loving and compassionate people as a result of their loss. They feel they live life more fully and have a deep gratitude for even the smallest blessings. Others have felt moved to work with those going through similar pain. Some now make immense contributions to their community, and on a personal level have grown into stronger, wiser people. Deep grief is something none of us wants to experience, but its great gift is that it can put us in touch with a wider humanity.

A beautiful box can store treasured memories.

My first baby dies at birth

The death of a baby is not part of any antenatal class. It is not spoken about in pregnancy books nor mentioned as a possibility by the doctor. As far as I was concerned, except in extremely rare circumstances, death at birth only happened in the last century to poor, malnourished women without medical attention.

It didn't happen to the babies of white, middle-class women like me, who ate all the right things, swam their laps and did their yoga in preparation for their drug-free birth.

The labour was a long, gruelling affair. Now I look back and wonder why I put myself through so many hours of torture. I vomited and slowly grew dehydrated and too distressed to cope. After twenty hours they anaesthetised me, cut me open and dragged her out, struggling for breath. Her lungs were coated with the sticky tar of her bowel lining: she had pooed in the womb in distress and breathed it in.

My partner Michael stayed with her through most of her eight-hour struggle for life. We were in a small regional hospital. By the time the neonatal retrieval team had her stabilised for the helicopter journey, they had just about given up hope for her survival. She died in the big city hospital in Michael's arms as he looked down on her with shock, love, guilt and bewilderment.

By the time I woke up, he had returned with her body. In that moment, wild horses would not have stopped me from taking her in my arms and holding her close. Every fibre of my wounded, exhausted body needed to feel the weight of that bundle, dead or alive. I needed to smell the scent of her and gaze for a long time on her features. I needed to unwrap her and examine her surgical wounds where they had cut open her chest to drain her lungs in a last desperate effort to save her life.

I needed to examine her legs, arms, fingers and feet and feel her soft downy hair between my fingers. It was exactly the honey-blonde colour of Michael's. I could not have put any of this into words at the time. I was lost somewhere in a dark fog of shock.

Years before I had been at this juncture of death and loss when my father died. I was dimly aware that a tidal wave was surging towards me, and there was nowhere to hide from its destruction.

My mother and sisters arrived a little later. I'd been hanging on, waiting for them, knowing I would be safe with them beside me. The beautiful, indelible bonds of family. I wanted them to see her. I unveiled her to show them her perfection, her chubbiness. I so desperately wanted to show her off. I was so proud of my creation, even in her lifelessness.

Michael held Layla tenderly, like he might a tiny angel with a broken wing. The silence was sacred—just the splash of water as we anointed her, baptising her with bathwater. Her body floated quietly on the surface. There was none of the startled thrashings of a newborn.

I could feel that roaring wave of grief in the distance and I knew with a sinking certainty it would pick me up and dump me with animal ferocity. Right then, however, I lay there and watched her still, silent face and knew I was beyond even the place of tears.

The caesarean added another level of shock. But it was a blessing in disguise as I was required to stay in hospital for four and a half days to recover, which meant I could spend time with Layla's body. It was warm and soft on the day after her death. But each night after that, my sister Alex would compose Layla's features, gently readying her again for the next day. She would then take her down to the hospital cold room where she would be kept overnight.

Some people might wonder why anyone would choose to experience such a thing. Better perhaps to hand the body over to a funeral director and cremate it a few days later. But I had learnt through my father's death that to avoid the reality of death was a dangerous and ultimately futile path. To me, tears were the ventilation of a breaking heart, the only tool I knew for the seemingly impossible task of healing. Mostly though, I needed so desperately to nurture her in whatever way I could. I needed a chance to be her mother. To be close to her, to see she had my snub nose and Michael's honey-blond hair, that her ears were tiny like mine, her feet exactly the shape of my mother's, that she had large hands like her father's. I thought her the most beautiful creature, but each day we felt the life force dissolve further and further from her body, preparing us for the inevitable relinquishing.

An unexpected death, a death 'too soon', is like a portal into an adjoining universe. There are no bearings. You move helplessly on currents of black despair and shock, confused by finding both beauty and a strange hysteria there. The beauty and sadness live like the rose and thorn.

A dead child seems to strike right to the heart of everyone, ripping us open, exposing us to the very core of our humanity. A great transference of love occurs until we are wrapped in a warm blanket of tenderness. Lying there in my wounded state, I recognised that the only way to give was to receive. Everybody was so desperately sorry, and their way of expressing that was to tend to any whim. My younger sister Rebecca gave me hand and foot massages. Others fought to bring beautiful food and make us eat. I wonder how people cope without this level of support. My older sister Alex quietly took rolls and rolls of film of Layla, the most precious photos in my collection.

Four days later, Michael and I walked towards the hospital exit, Layla snuggled against my chest, making people smile unaware as we passed. We had been released to attend a small family ceremony that afternoon, out into the obscenely bright sunshine of a February day, into a world that functioned as though nothing had happened. It had been arranged for us to take Layla's body home overnight, a practice not normally allowed. Her body should have been released into the care of a funeral home but our enlightened female funeral director had agreed to sign the papers so we could take her.

I sat alone in the bathroom at home holding Layla and a blackness descended. I thought about how it would be after everyone had gone home, after the flowers had died and the phone stopped ringing. This would be my future, a home without Layla. A slow sinking gloom took hold of my body, hunching my shoulders, her still form pressed against the aching cavity where once she thrived.

The ceremony began in the golden light of late afternoon in our rearranged living room. Michael exuded a kind of nobility as he spoke of our grief:

We believe that crying is part of what heals, a sign that you are in pain but also that the pain is dissolving. We both feel strongly that this ceremony is a symbol of letting go but it's also a new beginning. Life can't go back now to how it was before this happened. So life begins, in a sense, from here. There's a lot of pain and a different way of looking at the world. I feel hopeful that it actually softens and deepens us. It involves having everything we are going to have and not needing to sweep it away. Everybody in this room is affected in their own way. They go on a bit differently, changed. So she is an amazing little person.

Our doctor, Phil Steele, had come. We invited him to speak. He relayed the circumstances around the labour and birth and the efforts the teams of medicos made to save her. He spoke about the joy of helping bring children into the world and about the pain when they lose a newborn child.

Then he looked at us and spoke straight from the heart: 'Michael and Vanessa, I'm sorry that I did not help bring your child safely into this world. I share your grief that your life will never be blessed by the living presence of Layla.'

I'm sorry. The sound of those words sent a great rush of energy through my body, like all the anger and confusion around the circumstances of her death had their first release in the face of his humility. His quiet admission that even in the 21st century, we still have no absolute control over life and death.

Deep grief rips open the heart, rips us open to new levels of ourselves. There is an agony in grief but what people don't talk about is that there is also an ecstasy. A terrible loss is often met with a great outpouring of love from people. In that love a deep connection is felt with others. We are closer suddenly to the pulsing of humanity and the pain of humankind. We are connected to the eternal impermanence of all things but also more deeply connected to that other eternal force, God.

I am only one in a long line of women through the centuries who has lost her child at birth. It was not so long ago that parents who lost their babies in a Western hospital did not even get to glimpse them. The parents were advised not to see these babies who were then buried in mass, unmarked graves. The medical authorities believed it was better for parents to go home, forget and 'try for another one', as though that baby was replaceable.

Parents who have lost a baby are plunged into shock. They don't know what to do, what is allowed, the memories they might make to help with the grieving. They don't know how to arrange a funeral that will be meaningful and appropriate for them. At this time more than ever, they need the guidance of enlightened healthcare professionals and compassionate friends and family. Afterwards, they need the particular understanding that comes from people who have walked the same rock-strewn path.

Months later when asked how I was, I found myself saying I was on the edge of what feels bearable. Twice now, recently, I have washed up and over that cliff onto a tiny patch of shimmering sand. I have no fear anymore of the emotional pain I'm in. I just surrender to it or sob with a friend down the phone, or lie on my bed and let the pain wrack my body. I know from experience that if I let myself do that, in time, maybe fifteen minutes later, maybe four hours later, I will cycle back into the light. So I surrender to my sorrow now with great trust. Twice recently, in the depths of my despair, with tears streaming down my face and my voice almost broken, I have felt my heart start to resonate with joy.

In these moments I feel almost exultant in my pain, as though it is taking me to the deepest part of myself and somewhere setting me free. I understand it is my love which has taken me to this place of despair and my love that will guide me back. Layla's gifts have been extraordinary. This is perhaps her greatest.

Every so often, someone would gently suggest that perhaps I needed antidepressants. I always rejected the idea, knowing that grief and depression were different beasts, although the first can often lead to the second. I knew the source of my grief. The fact that sometimes I could still feel joy and laugh until I cried, to me, was a sign that this was not depression. I sensed that there was a wisdom emerging through the emotions. To anaesthetise them was to reject this source of wisdom. I knew I had to sit with and learn to endure my emotional distress.

There is no 'right' timeframe for grief; no predictable pattern within which it should all be played out. There is only the individual moving toward a future where nothing will ever look the same as it did before the death. Hopefully, a recognition that impermanence, change and loss are the nature of the universe, and acceptance of this, creates the state of grace within which our lives can be lived.

There are no words that heal, but not to receive those attempts is worse. There are no words of comfort, but the lone-liness of that void is such that we are desperate for anything anyone has to offer, no matter how clumsy. We want to feel hands reaching out even if they fail to hold us fully, even if they manage to hold us steady only for a fleeting moment.

I could always feel the difference between people who have experienced deep grief and those who have not. While they don't know *my* place they know *the* place and generally, they are not afraid to go there with you. *'Thank God,'* we cry when we meet others deeply in that place. *'Thank God they have known loss as well,'* we selfishly cry.

I am coming to understand that nothing will save me except myself. I have to go deep inside and find the place of silence. The place where nothing is touched by external events. Painful emotions can rise and fall on the surface but not permeate that place of peace. I think I am scared to sit and meditate, because it means sitting with my grief and to do that makes me agitated.

I remember Michael's words about heartbreak: 'What does it mean, this pain? What is it really but broken attachment, something longed for that never arrives or that is held closely but then lost?'

When I first lost Layla, I knew the expression 'Time heals', but secretly I was convinced some part of me would never get over losing her. Nowadays, even though there is still an absence where my seven-year-old daughter should be, I know there has been a healing. Not that a deep sadness won't always be there, but the scar tissue is strong now and will no longer tear under all but the most intense pressure.

I know the secret that as pain arises, it also falls. I also know the intensity of the grief for parents when they are in the thick of it. The feeling that they will never escape the pain, never resume a normal life.

Somehow, as a community, we have to offer parents and the family the life raft of our love and support. Within that, they may find a trust that there will be a healing, that at some point in the future, life will again hold some peace, even joy. They will no doubt be indelibly changed, but they will survive.

After Layla's death, I was sure I had lost the chance of ever becoming a mother again: I was nearly 40, Michael and I had separated, and Layla was gone. It was the bleakest time I can remember. It was impossible then to imagine the direction my life would take and that in the intervening years I would move from such intense grief to the state of grace I am now in as the mother of two living children.

Although subsequent children can never 'replace' the one that is lost, my two children, Raphael and Francesca, have been my saviours, as has their father James. They have returned joy to my life. I have an urge to celebrate my love for them often and to share it with anyone who will listen. This mother love is an ordinary thing, but to me it is something extraordinary. It's the tender wind that propels my existence now. That fills my days with unexpected glee and makes me pause often to offer up my gratitude to life. Layla's death has given me a deep appreciation of the gift of their lives. I take nothing for granted.

When it all comes down to it, to love deeply is to expose oneself to the possibility of profound loss. The deeper we love, the deeper we grieve. But this is life's challenge: to open ourselves wide and embrace everything life hurls at us. To smile at our destiny.

Vanessa Gorman

'My first baby dies at birth', an excerpt from *Layla's Story* by Vanessa Gorman, with kind permission of Penguin, Australia.

Acknowledging grief

Grief is a very individual experience, and the length of time needed to grieve may vary from a month to a lifetime. Differences in cultural expectations of an appropriate time-frame for grieving are important considerations when helping the bereaved. Comments such as 'I thought they would be over it by now' are inappropriate. The bereaved do not have a choice about lifting their grief or moving it on. In some countries widows wear black for at least a year after their husband's death, or even indefinitely, to signal their grief. For the rest of us, there are few signals.

The loss of a life partner, for instance, particularly after 40 or 50 years, is so devastating that for many their lives seem to fall apart. They literally feel there is no reason to get out of bed in the morning. That's why elderly partners often die within a few weeks or months of each other. One of the hardest things for them to deal with can be getting rid of their loved one's personal possessions, particularly their clothes, as they hold the scent of the person and are often the most tangible reminder of their presence. Some people appreciate offers of help. Others prefer to wait until later to deal with these details.

Grief can be debilitating, and can reduce the most energetic, organised person to a state of helplessness. For this reason any practical help you can give—such as meals, grocery shopping, making phone calls or child care—is hugely appreciated. Many people are so distressed they simply cannot be bothered or have no experience of feeding themselves. It all becomes too much effort. Having always had someone to eat with, the loneliness of sitting down by yourself can be overwhelming. A regular visit, say on a Sunday morning for breakfast or taking some favourite treat, can mean so much. Meals which can be easily reheated, like soups or stews, are also a good idea. In many communities people will make a roster and take it in turns to deliver a meal to someone in need.

Jan lost her husband in his late 60s. She went to grief counselling organised by the palliative care group in her area. Here, she found herself with other men and women who were recently bereaved. The comfort from sharing their most intimate fears and feelings was so reassuring and consoling for her, as was just realising she was not alone in her grief. As time went by the group started to go for walks together in the nearby national park. Sometimes they would visit beautiful gardens. As a result five of the women have formed a closely knit group and now get together on their own initiative and travel together on holiday. This support and companionship have given them a whole new lease of life.

However, life is not always like this, and so it's important to keep a close eye on someone who is suddenly left on their own. They may say they are fine, but behind closed doors, they may not be coping well. Some bereaved people find it impossible to reach out for help and may benefit from being encouraged to seek grief counselling.

As we see from Vanessa's description of her long journey through grief, it was vital that people reached out, however clumsily, to acknowledge the place she was in. We often worry that there's nothing we can say which can make a difference. Or we're concerned we might make things worse. But it is almost always better to say something rather than nothing. Even if we only manage to say, 'I am so sorry to hear about your loss. Is there anything I can do?' Don't be afraid to mention loved ones by name. They are still very much alive in the hearts of those left behind, and talking about them can be very comforting.

When Claire received the phone call that her mother had died, her immediate reaction was to get in the car and go to the ocean. It was a wild windy day on the deserted beach. Here, as time stood still, she felt free to pace beside the crashing surf and howl. She allowed herself to pace for a long while. Waves of emotion washed over her and were absorbed by the elements, until finally an exhausted peace descended. That's why many people find it helpful to be in nature and allow their grief to have physical expression and release.

Sending a few carefully chosen words in a letter or on a beautiful card can often be something that is treasured for years to come. It makes a huge difference to someone feeling isolated in their grief to know others are concerned about them. Sadly, letters of condolence are almost a lost art, but definitely worth reviving.

Here's an example: 'My heart goes out to you and all your family at this time of transformation, and I pray that you all may grow and benefit by all that he wished for you and all that you wish for each other. Life and love are forever and live in the morning dew, the evening sunset, the first smile of a baby, in nature and in the endless wonder of a young child. You are surrounded by love.'

It's worth being aware that as time goes by, anniversaries, birthdays or Christmas can be particularly challenging times for grieving people to face alone. At these times the support of family and friends is very important. It can help to buy a lovely picture frame that would appeal to the bereaved and then help them find a photo to place in it. Many a conversation can be started around simple actions such as these. It can help people re-engage with life when someone else shows an interest in the history of their relationship with the person who has died. Photographs can prompt reminiscing and the telling of many wonderful stories, all of which can bring comfort.

Losing my little son

My son Flynn entered this world at first light, as a soft rain was falling. He left in the early hours, in a raging storm. At both moments he was surrounded by love. He was here for seven years, seven days and six hours.

*

Five days before the end. The headache started again. I've taken you to hospital, a 50-minute drive. I'm not sure how I got here. Your older sister is beside you. She holds you tightly to her. Knowing. All of us knowing. We have done this before.

Scans are taken. We have another helicopter ride. Your dadda makes the tortuous two-hour drive to be with you as there's no room in the helicopter. He and I meet at the helipad and weep silent tears together. This time we may lose you, yet we live in hope. The symptoms are not as severe as last time, we say, over and over. More scans are taken then you are back in the ward. Your face beams as staff members recognise you. They come to say hello, all smiles for a favourite patient. But I notice a sadness in their faces to see you back. Dadda and I are called to the ward room, hoping, hoping. Doctors and nurses are waiting. Your brain scans are lit up on the wall. As we stare at the screen a voice says, 'There's nothing we can do. So sorry. So very sorry.'

We stare blankly at the screen, screaming silently with pain. The words resounding.

'How long?' I ask, and am told you have 'four or five days, a week maybe'. Our son is dying. *Oh, dear God. Our baby is dying.*

We are given time alone before returning to your bedside. When we join you, you look bright-eyed and bushy-tailed. Yet in spite of that mischievous twinkle in your eyes, we are to have you with us for only a few more days. Your sister and brothers arrive with their godmothers—all were there to see you enter this world and will be here with you as you depart.

There is such pain inside me as I watch their faces, each dealing with the shattering news, feeling their pain. You have been such a big part of their lives. I know that you will always be with them, watching over them. In your dadda's face I see utter despair: no more 'wuff-ups' in the morning; no more fluffy dragon to bid you sweet dreams; no more little boy to carry sleeping to his bed at night; no more sweet face that mirrors his own.

We are given a private room. Our time is precious. There are few distractions here. Many come to spend time with you. We watch the bewilderment in the faces of your little friends. We watch as each day your small body is able to function less and less. You say little. It's funny the things I remember, like the chair in that room. It is a bright blue reclining rocker. I spend a lot of time in that chair during those five precious days, with you in my arms, reading your favourite books including 'the little nutbrown hare who said to the big nutbrown hare, "I will love you to the moon and back" and the big nutbrown hare says to the little nutbrown hare "I will love you forever".' As the days pass I burn your face into my memory, clutch your body to mine, hold you tight and love you, just love you.

It's your last day with us, there's a storm brewing outside. You are in my arms. Everyone is here. It is the early hours of the morning. The trees lash against the windows and the wind howls. The kids gaze outside. They are so brave, as are you, my darling. So very, very brave. 'It's okay darling,' I say. 'You can go now. The angels are here.' Seven times I say that over the course of an hour, each time thinking you are taking your last breath.

'It's okay darling,' I say, as your big blue eyes look up into mine. You just look at me. There is no fear, just acceptance and a sense of peace. Then it happens. You come back no more.

A doctor enters the still room. He kindly leaves us with you. Your perfect seven-year-old body is gently lifted from my arms and placed on the bed. I watch as your godmothers lovingly bathe you and dress you in your favourite clothes. Finally you are wrapped in a special golden shawl. Your godmother stands at the end of the bed, weeping. It is her shawl. She will miss your weekend stays, your long walks on the beach, your hours of drawing together. She loved you and you, her.

We all stroke your hair and look down on your sweet face. Oh God, how can this be? I will not see my boy grow into a fine young man. I will not see you run another marathon. How can I never take you in my arms again?

We take you home. We have you for three more days. The following day our home is open to anyone who would like to sit with you quietly, to say their goodbyes, to light a candle, or to place a flower or a memento beside you. People want to give succour to our family, to thank us for letting them come, but I want to thank them, for letting us share our grief.

The day of your funeral finally arrives. It has been raining since the night you died, but today the sun is shining. Silently we all get ready. Your coffin is brought inside. It has been lovingly made by friends. You are lifted inside it by big, burly, weeping men, feeling helpless as they watch your family and friends' pain. Until now I have been in a daze—I think it was a kind of protection, helping me get through each day. But as I see you there, surrounded by your precious things, I see that it is real. And roses, so many roses. Your favourite flower. I feel a primal wail coming from somewhere so deep inside me. It is the voice of a terrible grief. The grief of a mother who has to bury her child.

We walk to the park at the end of our street. We spread out, holding hands, for strength.

You are placed on a trestle under the low, hanging branch of the old fig tree, the same branch where your dadda used to lift you up high, where you used to sit and feel on top of the world. Today, in the middle of the day, an owl sits on this branch, watching over you. Under you sits your beloved dog, Tillie, quiet as a mouse. The park is full to overflowing. We are only a small community, but so many have come to wish you goodbye. Your great and final gift to the community is to bring us all together in love. Adults and children alike have written you messages, which they place beside you in your coffin. The children are not afraid. They cover your coffin inside and out with your favourite stick-on twinkly stars. You look so beautiful, like an angel. Kath, your friend, is here, weeping. She will miss the time spent with you in her garden. It is Kath who gave you your love of roses.

Alex, your school principal, stands and speaks about a boy who suffered a stroke at the age of five and how you entered kindergarten on your first day, dragging your leg, your arm hanging limp at your side, a tube sticking out under your shirt through which you were fed. Alex speaks of your courage, your will and your sheer determination. How you recovered against great odds, and ran the kindergarten marathon, streaking ahead to first place. He speaks of the inspiration you gave.

Michael, your doctor and friend, sings 'Puff the Magic Dragon'. I call out for everyone to sing along, sing it loud, sing it loud for Flynn. Then our old family friend Elizabeth and all the school children, holding hands, form a circle around you to sing the 'Circle of Life' from *The Lion King*.

When we leave the park, a small group heads to the cemetery. Although this day is perfect, it has been wet all week. The water table is up and your grave is half-full of water.

After a simple poem, we turn away from the grave with your small coffin still sitting on the top, and walk away across the field. Our friend stays behind and lowers you into the earth.

*

My darling Flynny boy, oh, how I miss you! Six weeks and one day since you died, it seems like a lifetime, like it was yesterday, like it never happened. My spirit soars with you but my heart aches. Memories flood in and sometimes often overwhelm me. I want to grab them all to me and never let go. I'm here on the hill that overlooks the cemetery. I sit beside an old grave with a beautiful tall angel: 'Here lies George'. I often sit here and talk to George. From here I can see the mountain you wanted to climb. I can see you rolling down this hill with your friends, laughing all the way. From here I can see your grave. Tillie is with me today. She seems lost without you, I do believe she has gone a little mad. I believe I have gone a little mad too, and yet as I think that, I can feel you present, wrapping your arms around me. The birds are singing and there's a soft breeze blowing. I come and sit here with you and feel comforted, blessed that you chose me as your mother.

*

Nine years on I still feel Flynn's presence whenever I think of him. The pain remains, but there's a softness to it now. The years since his death have been a long and often painful journey. To lose one's child . . . Parents often tell me they cannot imagine what it would be like to lose a child. My response is, 'Don't even try.' There is no imagining what could even come close. Yet I give thanks every day for the gift of the seven years that Flynn was here with us, for the gift of being mother to this remarkable boy. Every day he is a light-filled being who watches over me, guides me, wraps me in his love, shines on me, and who has brought a divine presence into my life.

Shortly after his passing, I knew I had to make a journey. Flynn seemed to be pushing me. I returned to India, to the river Ganges. There I boarded a small row boat and set out into the middle of the river at dusk with a small lighted candle set among rose petals and marigolds. I placed it in the waters of the sacred river and watched it drift into the distance on the current. With my silent prayers and tears, I set my son free.

I live on my own in India now. I have built a small boutique hotel. It is Flynn's gift to me. Here I feel at peace. I take joy in the presence of all the children around me now, although previously, in my deepest grief, I avoided them. My broken heart is healing as I laugh and play with the children, take joy in their closeness and delight in their innocence. Flynn is sometimes here with us. I see him in the twinkle of a child's eye or in the smile of another. In their laughter I hear him. It brings immense joy to my heart, and for this I give thanks.

Lulu Exton Pery

Creativity in grief

Sitting in the company of death may seem an unusual time to consider being creative, but as author Julia Cameron says, 'creativity—like human life itself—begins in darkness'. In our darkest moments, if we allow our creative selves expression, we can often touch something far greater than ourselves and begin to let the light in. Everyone is an artist. Expressing yourself creatively is your birthright and gives voice to your soul.

If you have a terminal illness, you might want to gather family and friends together to decorate your coffin. Decorating a coffin together allows people to open up to tender areas rarely shared, permitting profound insights and connections. We all have unique and valuable ways of expressing ourselves, so don't be anxious about being creative. Simply create from your heart and it will bring love and healing, and encourage others to dare to do the same.

If you know someone who is dying, you might like to start creating something to honour them, such as a patchwork quilt, a photomontage of their life, video footage of their recollections, or a collection of their life stories to be bound into a book. You may include the dying person in the process if they have enough energy. Sometimes they already know what they want done, as with Trish for her wedding. Creative projects are special because they continue to capture something precious about a loved one, even after they are gone. The lovely thing is they may become family heirlooms, while also being healing. We see in Fran's story how Maggie and her family created the quilt as a work in progress for future generations to contribute to.

After someone has died it can be challenging to organise a more creative funeral. Legal and other requirements may seem to threaten the very tenuous hold you want to retain with your loved one. However, to bring an unadorned coffin, like a blank canvas, into a home to decorate, where family and friends can talk about the loved one while creatively expressing their love, can bring laughter and light to all, including little children, as a unique moment is shared. Tiny children's handprints adorning a coffin will allow them partnership in a mighty experience.

Liz, an 85-year-old mum, would definitely have loved the TR3 Triumph racing car painted onto her coffin for her farewell ride. She'd spent a number of years in Ghana where unique coffins honour the individuality of the person buried inside, and was an inaugural member of the Ghana Rally Club. So this was a perfect depiction of her life. The men in the family loved creating her car, and people were asked to create their own personal design of what she meant to them. These were made into stickers that were placed on the car.

The racing theme was extended when her son collected special music in her honour, then put together a CD entitled 'Liz's last burn-out'. It lightened the pain of losing her, and he was able to watch people line up to sign her coffin before it was wheeled into the chapel to the beat of a Ghanaian drummer. Her family felt certain she would have said, 'What a perfect way to say farewell.'

There are so many challenges and opportunities around death. At first it may seem incredibly daunting to sit with a little seven-year-old boy who has just lost his father to AIDS, and attempt to find a way to offer some solace. Getting out a large sheet of paper, coloured pencils and paint, and starting a conversation through drawing which lasts all day, talking about his magical father, what he did and what he has left behind, allowed joy to shine through the sadness (see page 30).

Supporting this same little boy to become involved in the funeral arrangements—by tying ribbons with a note to seedlings, for everyone to plant and nurture, in memory of his father— brought an unforgettable connection. Precious recollections will remain in the hearts of the many who attended that funeral. People took away memories of a small purposeful child reaching into his father's coffin to lay across his heart his treasured painting, covered in crystals, clothes pegs and gumnuts, symbolic of the things he wanted his father to travel with to heaven.

When someone finds themselves alone in an empty house resonating with the remembered sounds of their loved one of 50 years, can there be a way to attempt to alleviate their pain? It can take courage to ask for a handful of ashes to add to a portrait to be painted of their loved one; the day Trypheyna returned with a painting, which held the essence of her father John, to keep Liz, her mother, company, Liz's radiant smile was reward enough. A gift of this sort will be treasured for years.

Finding new ways of remembering someone who has died can be very important in a world where physical markers of a person's life, such as grave sites, are becoming less common. You may choose to write an obituary for the newspaper, or set up an interactive blog on the internet dedicated to your loved one. This way others can add photos and writings about them, making it a shared experience.

Coffins do not need to be traditional oblong boxes. Desiree, whose grandparents were Swedish, was sent off in a canary-yellow Viking boat. Courses are now being held to encourage people to have fun making their own coffins. They can double as bookcases, blanket boxes and other useful household furniture.

Those not interested in carpentry can buy a plain coffin and create their own, or another's, life story in photos on it or in it.

Everyone needs a chance to express their feelings creatively. There are untold ways for this to be done, such as through music, flowers, craft, sculpture, sewing, writing and performing. Many people sing or play a favourite piece at the funeral, or use flowers as Claire's family did when they made a magnificent Tahitian lei for her father's coffin to which her mother added a touching bunch of forget-me-nots.

Being in the presence of death shifts your focus, so it's a perfect time to open up to the unknown and unexpected. Trusting your inner guidance and expressing yourself creatively can take you to unimagined places of healing.

A unique coffin can reflect your loved one's passion or talent in life.

My little boy sensed
his death

My firstborn son, Benjaya (pronounced Benj-I-a), was one of the first babies to be born in water in England. It was an excruciatingly painful, yet exquisitely empowering entry into motherhood. The venue was an attic in my family home which had been used for healing work for many years.

The birth experience was a sacred initiation to me. My son swam into life at dawn, and as he was lifted from the warm water into my arms, his big brown almond-shaped eyes connected with mine and my world stood still. This magical moment was captured in a photograph that encircled the world the following day in newspapers with headlines such as 'The joy and miracle of birth', and was reported on television.

Much interest in water birth ensued and soon my husband, Abel, and I set up a company to cope with the prolific requests for information. We designed and built portable birthing tubs to make water birth widely available and began lecturing on the subject all around Britain. Benjaya went with us and was always the star of the show.

He was a charismatic child: handsome, agile, full of life and, at times, wise beyond his years. I had a sense that his bigness was trapped within his small child's body, and that he was often frustrated by his desire to be free from its restrictions. Abel and I saw him as our teacher, showing us how to love unconditionally.

My mother, M'haletta, and I led workshops for midwives on holistic childbirth, and always included a session on death. We sometimes spoke about our desire to work more closely with death, and she tentatively voiced her awareness that someone within our family was preparing on some level to die. She was right.

My nightmare began on a weekend train journey to London. Benjaya, now five, was staying at home with Abel as I was to be the key speaker at a seminar about 'ideal birth'. I was newly pregnant and feeling very sick, but when I reached Paddington station in London I felt much sicker. Between train announcements I could hear, 'Will Mrs B'Hahn go to the information desk'. There I was told gruffly to phone my husband.

Abel's voice was tight and emotionless. 'Sorry to drag you off the platform but you must come home on the next train.'

Noise . . . commotion . . . I can't hear properly . . .

'It's Benjaya, he's fallen in the river. We don't know if he's alright, he's been taken to hospital.'

And then we were cut off.

My brain was foggy. I could hardly stand with the shock. But I *had* to move and think. In a stupor I found a train, which seemed to take years to snail its way home. No-one offered a kind word to quell my obvious distress. I was terrified that my sweet Benjaya, so active in his perfect body, would live but brain-damaged. I scribbled in my diary, attempting to connect with sanity:

I need to love and let go of my fear. I mustn't blame Abel. Don't think about what might be. Come back to the now. What is, is. What will be, will be. I AM LOVE. I LOVE BENJAYA AND RELEASE HIM TO WHATEVER IS BEST FOR HIM. I LOVE ABEL. I LOVE OUR NEW GROWING BABY. Benjaya, wherever you are, I am with you and am sending you love for your healing process, be that to live or die peacefully. May the will of God be done.

At my station the platform was flanked by police—it all seemed impossibly unreal. I nodded feebly as one policeman stated, 'You're Carmella, aren't you?'

I was ushered into a stark office where a blonde police-woman sat me down and spoke these indelible words into my daze: 'There's no easy way to say this, Mrs B'Hahn, but we found your son's body in the river this evening. We thought you'd want to know as soon as possible. Your husband's at home, we'll take you there.'

And so my son, born so beautifully in a pool of water, had died that day by slipping into a pool in the river and been washed away. No ashes to ashes, dust to dust for him. The following day it hit the news and flowers and cards began filling the house, which now had the same hushed aura about it as the day he was born. The heart-rending emotional pain equalled the physical pain of bringing him into the world. The song sung to Benjaya when he was six months old at his blessing cere-mony had come true:

The river is flowing, flowing and growing,
The river is flowing down to the sea.
Mother Earth carry me, a child I will always be,
Mother Earth carry me back to the sea.

The human me was shocked to the core, incapable of making a cup of tea, dazed and physically sick. And yet, into that wretched abyss a light was shining all the time—sometimes glimmering, sometimes dazzling. It was present, by no conscious thought of my own, and seemed to emanate from me as if it was another aspect of my self. It felt as if the human me was wither-ing, but this light or spirit flatly refused to die.

Many thoughts and memories arose in those first raw days, which had the effect of expanding the light place within and supporting my rock-solid certainty that Benjaya's death had been a perfectly orchestrated finale. Despite my anguish, from the moment I heard the word 'river' I accepted my son's fate. No anger showed its face and no voice within me ever attempted to make his death wrong. It simply was what life had dealt us and it hurt like hell.

Throughout my life I have 'heard' guidance in my head. Back when I was eight months pregnant with Benjaya, I was sitting with a group of people when suddenly I felt choked with an emotion that was not my own. I knew, as crazy as it may seem, that if I opened my mouth my child-to-be would speak. I took the plunge and allowed the words to come spilling out:

> You may not think that we have fear here, but I am afraid. Birth to me and to those with me is like a death—death to who I really am. Just as there is death in birth, so there is birth in death. Please remember this and keep me conscious of who I am when I come.

Five and a half years later these words echoed into my anguish and gave some comfort—there is birth in death. Together with the agony, I felt an awe-filled wonder at the great mystery of death. In poet Christopher Fry's words, this was 'the longest stride of soul' I had ever taken. The sense of living another sacred initiation equal to that of birth was often with me, but because I found this to be too much for most people to comprehend, I kept it mostly to myself. Lao Tzu said, 'What the caterpillar calls the end of the world, the master calls the butterfly.' I craved to talk butterfly-speak but, in the face of death, realised few could speak the language.

The media was portraying the mass consciousness about this kind of death: 'A tragic accident and cruel loss of life'. There was no room for the balance of feelings I experienced or for a positive word about a five year old's fullness of life and meaningful finale. I wanted to shout from a soapbox: 'Why can't you see that feeling heartache doesn't make death wrong or the life lived wasted because it was short? Tell me why my boy's death was not as natural and as sacred as his birth?'

It soon became obvious to me that Benjaya had subconsciously known he was going to die young. He often initiated conversations about death and was particularly fascinated with the subject. He asked, 'When I die will I meet your old cat?' and 'Who will my mother be when I come back again?' His favourite book was one about the world's spiritual traditions and he insisted that we read a page about reincarnation repeatedly. He started to give away his precious toys weeks before he died and wanted to stay in with me more, which was completely out of character. He even drew a skull-and-crossbones flag, and drowned his Lego pirates in a blue silk river. I took a photograph of that river with its tiny china swan swimming towards the bridge. (His body had floated downstream to a bridge where it was found in the position of the swan.) He made me everlasting paper flowers and said, 'Don't get your hopes up Mum, I'm not going into the next class, I've got another school I need to go to.' Then he said, 'I'm not going swimming on Sunday but I don't know why.' He died that Friday.

We were later told of other thought-provoking events involving water that occurred the week of Benjaya's death. His friend, Nikhil, became obsessed with water and played a game of repeatedly drowning his dolls and bringing them back to life. When told of Benjaya's death he said, 'That's alright, it doesn't matter.'

Benjaya's cousin, Sommer, was in India with my mother when he died, playing a daily game of pretending to drown. 'Do you think people will think I'm dead?' she asked my mother. 'Don't let them save me, will you?' (Why did she not want to be saved?) Then she asked, 'Who would you rather have die, Benjaya or Carmella?'

'Carmella,' answered my mother, 'because that is what she would wish.'

And yet another. The day Benjaya died, Tim Coombes, who was living a long way away from our home in Devon, had sudden chest pain, a terrible sense of heaviness and an image of a small boy slipping into deep water while clambering down a bank. Tim sobbed and clutched his son, thinking it could be a premonition of his death. We first met Tim months later after he had moved to Devon to become a teacher at Benjaya's school. I would have met him the day of his premonition had I made it to the conference on ideal birth where Tim discovered the reason for the key speaker's absence.

We had Benjaya's body cremated as we thought that fire was the most appropriate element for him. Collecting the ashes and holding the remains of my boy's body in a brown plastic urn was torturous. His big brown eyes were in white bits in my hands. How could I integrate that reality? And yet into the anguish the light still shone in the form of a voice saying, 'Don't cry Mummy, it's only my body!'

The grieving process was compounded three months after Benjaya's death by the loss of the baby I was carrying, followed later by a second miscarriage. My study of death and my belief systems about the afterlife certainly softened the process, but as time ticked by and friends went back to their normal lives, I did not escape the nitty-gritty process of grief taking its course. I realised that shock is clever. It brings with it protective veils to shield us from the brutal truth of loss, but as time passes and shock recedes, the veils thin and blow in the wind, bringing gusts of the physical finality of death. *Oh my God, I'm NEVER, EVER going to see my boy again* . . . it began to sink in. There was an overwhelming feeling of something missing, as if a limb had been severed. Lack screamed from every corner; no small shoes next to mine, no crumbs in the bed, no place at the table, and just a space where his car seat used to be. Space . . . silence . . . gaps . . . holes. Easter without Easter eggs, summer without buckets and spades, Christmas with no stocking to fill, and his birthday without him. This was the daily reality of my grief.

I realised that the literature on grieving that places it on a timeline with prescribed steps back to normal functioning was totally at odds with my experience. My grieving was like a spiral on which I annually revisited the same anniversaries, memories and triggers that would cause me to re-live the loss. Each turn of the spiral carried less intensity than the tighter twist of the year before. Rehabilitation and loving support are needed for a long, long time.

Synchronicities kept coming. The mother of Nikhil, who had been drowning his dolls, told us that he had been singing, 'Spread your rainbow wings and fly into forever . . . ', a song we had sung at the funeral/celebration that he had not attended. When asked how he knew the song he said, 'It just was.' Another little boy, Sol, was asleep on his mother's lap as she was meditating. When he woke, Sol told her he had been dreaming that Benjaya was alive and had come here to talk to her. He said, 'It was when the morning owls came.' They did not know that Benjaya had a passion for owls.

Butterflies and pennies became a source of solace. Since a bronze butterfly swooped down over the coffin at Benjaya's cremation, I have associated this symbol with him. When facilitating a 'Shedding Light on Death' workshop, I invited the presence of all our loved ones who had died. It was then that a large coloured butterfly descended to dance in circles around me. Everyone noticed that it was only me it wanted. Benjaya's favourite song was called 'Magic Penny' and since he died pennies have manifested all over my path, sometimes in startling ways. I once found a penny down my bed after dreaming about him. One morning as I was wrestling with how to write about synchronicity, my cat gave a loud screeching cough. Following the angle of her nose I saw not a mouse or a bird, but an earth-streaked penny on the ground between her paws.

A major realisation for me during this time of loss was this: individual events and synchronicities seem unconnected and senseless if we are looking at them in isolation. When we shift our perspective to an overview and question how the parts might fit together as a whole, a coherent picture emerges, allowing our relationship with those parts to transform.

There are some questions that I have been asked repeatedly since Benjaya's death, now answered in my first book *Benjaya's Gifts*. I would like to share and expand the answers to two of those questions.

Why do you think this happened to you?

The whole scenario of Benjaya's birth, life and death seems like an unfinished giant jigsaw puzzle. Some pieces show recognisable parts of the picture and the logical mind can fit them together. Likewise, I can say that the water birth fits with the water death. Benjaya's interest in death and the premonitions could fit with his early departure, and my studies of the subject and desire to work with death fit with experiencing it firsthand. I could say that Benjaya came to start a trend in water birth, to teach us about holistic birth, love and death.

I could say that the next baby (who later died) graced me with the lifeline of motherhood when I was first facing Benjaya's death. Some jigsaw pieces, however, are deceptive. Like this one, they seem to match perfectly at the time, but then another part of the picture just won't fit, so you have to concede that this piece doesn't belong there after all and remove it.

And what about the expanse of blue sky that boggles the mind with its challenging sameness? We can go only so far with our powers of understanding; to attempt to understand everything is futile. With the second miscarriage I was plunged into my blue sky—into an agony of failure because I could not understand why this was happening to me. 'Three deaths is too much to bear' was my daily affirmation. It took a while of weeping and wailing before I remembered that the best way of completing a jigsaw is sometimes to leave it alone. Either someone else will put the last pieces in, or we will go back to it with a changed attitude and the pieces will miraculously fall into place. Why that happens is a mystery.

Why are you so sure that Benjaya's death was not an accident?

My initial response on hearing of Benjaya's death was an instant and inexplicable sense of rightness—catastrophic to my senses, but right. This was not a reasoned strategy for coping but a resonance on some profound level with the drama that was playing itself out, as if I knew deep down that this was in our script.

Benjaya, of course, did not consciously jump into the river to his destined fate. Witnessed by two young friends, he fell while clambering down a riverbank as a branch snapped underfoot. This we call 'an accident'. My English dictionary defines an accident as 'an *unforeseen* event or occurrence happening unexpectedly by chance'. But it *was* foreseen, so where does that leave our language and comprehension of the nature of reality? Can any one of us explain how the stick knew to break? Premonitions and accidents don't mix, do they? And if his death was not an accident, what then of the apparent accidents of others? What if they were also foreseen events but the premonitions had simply not been shared? And would we grieve differently if we knew for certain that our losses made sense in the context of an overall plan or divine design?

There are so many questions; so much blue sky. Now, in an attempt to put a piece of sky in place, I will share one of my hypotheses, which may or may not fit.

I think that although human beings have free will, we may well operate within the limits of a wide and beneficial life blueprint, which interacts and dovetails with the blueprints of others. I imagine that we have unconscious awareness of our blueprint that holds the pattern for our greatest potential, and perhaps have by some yet-to-be-discovered process given it the seal of our approval. The humble caterpillar holds the blueprint of a butterfly, so it's not too far-fetched to imagine that humans have an equally miraculous potential in this world. We do, however, tend to romanticise the caterpillar's transformation into a butterfly. Scientists have recorded a screaming sound from the cocoon as the butterfly is formed and then struggles to break out of its prison. My process has been similar and I feel as if I have emerged with bright wings from the darkest place I could have imagined.

In 1993 I gave birth in water to a second son, Asher, with big brown almond-shaped eyes. Motherhood did not die as I had feared and my days are now spent helping others as a bereavement counsellor, workshop leader, and writer on the topic of how to raise a phoenix from the ashes of life's hellish fires. This work, along with the transformation that has occurred in British birthing practices, is my first son's legacy.

Carmella B'Hahn

'My little boy sensed his death' is adapted from *Mourning Has Broken: Learning from the wisdom of adversity* by Carmella B'Hahn, with kind permission of Crucible Publishers, Bath, UK.

Premonitions and insights

There appears to be overwhelming evidence that intuition and clairvoyance become more highly attuned around death. Those who work in the field of death and dying talk about how even people who are killed or die suddenly often know they are going to die. Some have been aware of it for a few weeks before their death occurs. At funerals, family and friends frequently mention situations that indicate the person was saying goodbye, or conveying an important message, somehow sensing they wouldn't get another opportunity.

Peter Lalor, with a beautiful young family to live for, had a dream in which he was given the date of his death. Throughout his illness and the process of his dying he was unafraid of what was to come.

Carmella shows us that little Benjaya, even at five years old, sensed he was going to die. He often initiated conversations about death, playing at drowning his Lego pirates, asking questions such as 'When I die will I meet your old cat?' and 'Who will my mother be when I come back again?' and then giving away his precious toys. He repeatedly insisted she read to him about reincarnation and, although it was out of character, he wanted to spend all his time with her. He even said to her, 'Don't get your hopes up Mum, I'm not going into the next class, I've got another school I need to go to', finally telling her, 'I'm not going swimming on Sunday but I don't know why'. He died that Friday. These are profoundly wise words from a little soul, alerting us to remain aware at all times to what our loved ones are really telling us.

In the case of Trish's death an intuitive voice instructed her family that everything should be ready in case a wedding needed to happen in a hurry, allowing her to marry her partner, and so her last wish was granted.

Three nights before her partner Greg died, Jenny was lying on the sofa, reading, next to his hospital bed, when she saw a shadow move. On looking up she saw two people standing at the door behind his bed. She couldn't see their faces, just their figures. They walked up to the side of his bed where he was asleep and stood on either side of him. One stroked his head, and the other his shoulder. She still couldn't see what they looked like. She heard them say to him, 'We're here and we will wait until you are ready.' She knew they were telling her, 'He'll be okay. We will be his escorts. He will be safe.' Many people talk of a comforting presence surrounding the dying that has allowed them to feel safe to let go of their loved ones, as is illustrated in a number of the stories. Maggie experienced a powerful connection over the last two nights before her mother Fran died with the faces of those who appeared to support her mother into the spirit world. In Angela and Tony's story, they experienced a sense of relief when they saw each of their deceased fathers there to support their dying daughter Anna on her journey. Even animals sense the illness and eventual departure of those they love, as shown by the cat Danny Boy in Barry's story.

Communication happens in many unexpected ways and it helps to be open to it. Gail, a community nurse, was never able to talk with a young man she helped nurse in his last few days because he was in a coma. Hearing he had died, the nurse called his home and found herself listening to a recorded message from the young man who had just died. She left her own message, saying, 'You have the most beautiful voice. I never heard it before. I am so happy to have heard you.' She never had a chance to know this man she had been nursing, and yet by other means he spoke to her.

Damini watched her friend die gradually from cancer. After the funeral, she told her friends she didn't want to die slowly but instead 'wanted to die instantly, in something like a plane crash'. The following week she and some friends were at a small airfield to take a flight to see the countryside from the air. Damini had come along to look after the son of her girl-friend while the others all went on the flight. At the last minute the little boy threw a tantrum, pleading with his mother not to go. She tried to pacify him but, seeing his distress, decided she couldn't go. Damini took the opportunity to go for a ride herself. Shortly after take-off the plane's engine showed signs of trouble. The pilot turned it around, heading back to land at the airport, but the plane crashed. The pilot and Damini were killed instantly. The two rear passengers were badly injured but survived. Do we call these things into our lives, or are we in tune with our intuition or inner knowing?

It's never too late

At the beginning of this book, 'The magic of a dying wish' tells Trish's story. Natasha's story 'It's never too late' now gives a postscript to this story.

*

Death is not just an ending but also the beginning of something new. Death informs life as much as life informs death. Nature teaches us that something must die in order for the new to be born and death's gifts are often found in unexpected places.

Being adopted is something I have known about for as long as I can remember, but I had always wondered who my birth family were.

Over the years, even though I had the most wonderful childhood, I always felt something was missing. I often tried to fill this void but the closest thing to inner peace for me was having my first child at a young age.

A few times I had wanted to search for my birth mother but somehow did not feel worthy of her. Even though I know it is not necessarily true in adoption cases, I still felt somehow it was my fault and that I was unworthy of this person's love.

After becoming ill with a brain tumour (I found later my journey with cancer coincided exactly with my mother's), I needed to discover where I came from and who my birth family was. I managed to find the first identifying information about myself and my birth mother. But due to my illness, I also felt this was enough. I was already feeling low and knew that if I was rejected I wouldn't have been able to cope. So I decided to leave things as they were and be happy that at least I had this information.

Sometime later I received a letter from the adoption services asking if I knew the whereabouts of Natasha Whenan. They said they had a relative who was searching for her. Of course I was curious. Without hesitation, but nervous and excited, I rang the department. The lady checked out all my details to make sure I was the Natasha she was looking for, which of course I was.

Then there was a pause. The voice on the other end seemed slightly troubled. She made sure I was not alone to hear this information, then told me my birth family wanted to get in touch. I was so excited. Could this be what I had wanted all this time? She went on to tell me my birth mother, Trish, had died four months earlier.

I was speechless. I think she could sense it. She then told me about Trypheyna and Alex (my aunt and uncle) and that I had a younger brother. She said that they were anxious to meet or have contact. I needed time to take this in, finding my birth mother and losing her all at the same time. I told her they could write to me.

A few days later a letter arrived. I felt overwhelmed with emotion and could hardly open it. Inside was a photo of my birth mother with her husband whom she married thirty-six hours before her death. I felt overwhelmed with emotions and read the letter over and over again, trying to take it all in. It was so comforting. I knew then that I wanted to find out more. I tried to write but the words just wouldn't come. After a while

I decided I would phone them and if this didn't work, then I would let it drop.

The phone call was amazing. Trypheyna was so welcoming. There and then I knew this call would change my life. We talked for hours. Then we arranged for my brother to call me the next night. I was afraid that it was going to be harder to speak with Kristian but I needn't have worried; we talked for a long time, as if we had known each other all our lives. I think our mother would have been so happy.

We began making arrangements to meet. In a few days they had me booked on a flight to Sydney. I was going to meet everyone, taking my youngest daughter Xsara with me. I was so nervous. The flight in some ways went too fast and in other ways not fast enough. Xsara and I walked off the plane and there was my mum's family.

They welcomed me and the empty feeling I had carried for so many years started to disappear. We shared so many things over that short time. I visited my mother's grave with Kristian and felt a strange sense of self that I had never felt before. It was a feeling beyond words.

When I arrived I was greeted by someone else's family and when I left I was farewelled by my own. I don't know how I am meant to feel about the death of a woman I had never met, but I do know she gave me the gift of life. In her death she gave me the gift of her family and the blessing of getting to know her through my brother. I thank her so much for this and know she would be happy for us all.

Natasha Burns

The gift of humour

As Creative Director of The Humour Foundation charity, I'd like to share my perspective on death and dying. Our organisation contributes to those in medical care through humour, based on the theory that 'Humans + Humour = Humanity'.

We have 57 'Clown Doctors' who work in general and children's hospitals, palliative care facilities and nursing homes. While children are our main focus we treat all carbon life forms!

In the ten years The Humour Foundation has been doing clown rounds, our Clown Doctors have spent time with many adults and children in the closing stages of their lives. We share what is sometimes considered an unconventional view of life and death, where humour plays a vital role in helping patients and loved ones deal with the end of their lives.

I do not see our culture helping us deal well with death. We expect our children and other family members will live long fruitful lives. Nothing else is acceptable. As a humble clown, I witness children coping with dying better than most adults. They don't carry the baggage—of financial worries, dysfunctional relationships, fear, regret or guilt—that grown-ups accumulate over a lifetime. Children live in the moment.

I can still see Liz, a nine year old, in the final stages of her illness, sixteen hours before her death. Celebrating her birthday with her family and two ukulele-playing Clown Doctors, she harnessed enough life energy to complain that her brother had a bigger helping of her own birthday cake than she did. Now that's living in the moment!

I remember Hope, only four years old. She had spent three years of her life struggling with cancer, and she didn't like being the centre of attention. Although we were constant visitors, she preferred to watch us clowns interacting with each other or somebody else in the ward. What she loved most was getting a laugh or a happy response from her dad, who was distraught with seeing his beloved daughter suffer. Clearly a gentle and emotional man, he often looked haggard and sad. Hope loved seeing a smile on his face, and took an almost maternal interest in the mental state of her grieving father. Perhaps she knew she wasn't long for this world, and had developed a sense of maturity far beyond her tender years.

I visited another little girl in intensive care who had fallen into a coma after tumbling backwards off a low fence. Doctors told her family she was unlikely to recover. Fiercely determined not to accept this diagnosis, her grandmother prayed hard for her granddaughter's recovery. She had lost her own mother the week before, and was determined not to lose her grandchild as well. On my return, two days later, the little girl had woken up and was asking for her mother. So miracles can happen.

Then there was Naomi, now nine years old. She was back in hospital after a bone marrow transplant from her mum. She had been in remission for two years. The cancer had returned in a very aggressive way and the prognosis was not good. This was tragic for her devoted parents. Her mum and dad had tried so hard to save her, dealing with infections, a low blood count and her very fragile immune system. It seemed such a short time she had been out of hospital, and now she was back in her old room, being cared for, while her short life ebbed away.

She died in the early hours of the morning. Later that day, her parents came back to thank the medical staff and collect her things. Tidying up her bed they discovered a small note under her pillow addressed to them. It read, 'If you two look after each other as well as you have looked after me over these years, you'll both be fine'. She was anxious that in their grief they did not neglect their own relationship. Wise advice from one so young.

We often seem to spend time papering up the cracks, in total denial about what is really happening, even when someone has already lived a long life.

Once, while sitting in the office of a palliative care doctor debriefing after our clown round, the phone rang. A distressed wife was pleading with him to take her husband out of the hospice and put him back into hospital for more invasive surgery. Even after explaining that her husband did not wish to leave the hospice, that he was comfortable and his pain management under control, the doctor had a very difficult job convincing her. She didn't think it acceptable to prepare for a calm and peaceful death. She didn't want him to 'give up'. My heart went out to her, although I couldn't help wondering if she was really helping him.

The two most important events in our lives are birth and death. Our arrival is heralded with excitement and fanfare. Flowers, cards, well-wishers and family crowd around the crib. Maternity wards are full of anticipation and excitement. Although there is always a risk of death, it is generally a happy place to work.

Contrast this with a hospice, which deals with people at the end of life's journey. Very often a sense of dread can prevail on entering the building, despite the committed and caring staff. It's a place which deals with grief, pain and suffering, both for those about to leave, and family and friends left behind. Daily, staff often deal with sick, angry depressed people. The burn-out rate is high.

The Humour Foundation believed it could make a difference by introducing Clown Doctors to brighten the lives of patients, families and staff. Cautiously, always consulting staff and asking patient or family permission, we started to engage them to create fun and laughter. Thankful relatives sent grateful letters. They loved seeing their nearest and dearest laughing and singing, sometimes only hours before they died.

Initially our experience was mainly with children in palliative care. It has been heart-warming to bring so much joy to so many children at the end of their lives. Now we would like to find ways to extend this support to the dying of all ages. By bringing joy and laughter into the equation, and taking a more adventurous approach, it benefits all concerned, particularly the wonderful caring staff.

Naturally, as a clown I do tend to wear rose-coloured glasses. But I believe it is up to each of us to create the changes we would like for our own dying. As Ghandi said 'We must be the change we wish to see.'

So my advice is to prepare yourself as soon as possible to forgive the trespasses of others. Let go of the wrongs you feel others have done to you. Give up those controlling tendencies, lighten up a little and smell the roses. Take as little baggage as possible, head towards the departure lounge and embrace the inevitability of death, and make this the biggest event since your birth—bon voyage!

Jean-Paul Bell

Tony laughing with 'St Peter' at his wake
(see also page 85).

Further reading

We read to know we are not alone, understanding another's journey connects us. These books range from supportive and 'how to' to an insightful novel. Some are not specifically about death but have helpful insights relating to issues which can culminate in death, and about people at risk of suicide and those suffering from mental illness. Other books relate directly to the people whose stories are in this book.

Anastasios, A., *Dying to Know: Bringing death to life*, Pilotlight, Australia, 2007

B'Hahn, C., *Mourning has Broken: Learning from the wisdom of adversity*, Crucible Publishers, 2002

B'Hahn, M. & C., *Benjaya's Gifts: An astonishing true life drama highlighting the unlimited power of the spirit*, Hazelwood Press, 1996

Cameron, J., *The Artist's Way: A spiritual guide to higher creativity*, Penguin, 2002

Deveson, A., *Tell Me I'm Here*, Penguin, 1998

Donaghy, B., *Anna's Story: A teenage life destroyed, a family devastated*, HarperCollins, 1996 (revised edn 2006)

——*Leaving Early: Youth suicide: the horror, the heartbreak, the hope*, Harper Health, 1997

Garner, H., *The Spare Room*, Text Publishing, 2008

Gorman, V., *Layla's Story: A memoir of sex, love, loss and longing*, Penguin, 2005

Hamilton, M., *What Men Don't Talk About*, Penguin, 2006

Hender, M., *Saying Goodbye: Stories of caring for the dying*, ABC Books, Australia, 2004

Kuhl MD, D., *What Dying People Want: Practical wisdom for the end of life*, PublicAffairs, 2003

Larkins, R., *Funeral Rights: What the Australian 'death-care' industry doesn't want you to know*, Penguin, 2007

Lee, Dr E., *A Good Death: A guide for patients and carers facing terminal illness at home*, Rosendale, 1995

Levine, S., *A Year to Live: How to live this year as if it were your last*, Random House, 1998

McKissock, M. & D., *Coping with Grief*, Penguin, 2006

Molloy, Dr W. & Mepham, V., *Let Me Decide: The health care directive that speaks when you can't*, Penguin, 1992

Munro, L., *The Do-It-Yourself Funeral Book*, Bellingen Shire Bereavement Service NSW, Australia, 2001

Myers, E., *When Parents Die: A guide for adults*, Penguin, 1997

Redfern Legal Centre, *Rest Assured: A legal guide to wills, estates and funerals* (4th edn), Redfern Legal Centre Publishing, Australia, 2005

Reoch, R., *Dying Well: A holistic guide for the dying and their carers*, Gaia Books, London, 1997

Stanton, R., *When Your Partner Dies*, Allen & Unwin, 1999

UK Natural Death Centre, *The Natural Death Handbook* (4th edn), 2003

Vercoe, E. & Abramwoski K., *The Grief Book: Strategies for young people*, Black Dog Books, 2004

Wakely, M., *Sweet Sorrow: A beginner's guide to death*, Melbourne University Press, 2008

Walsh, R., *Great Australian Eulogies*, Allen & Unwin, 2008

Yalom, I.D., *Staring at the Sun*, Jossey-Bass, 2008

Helpful websites and contacts

Alzheimer's

Australia—www.alzheimers.org.au

NZ—www.alzheimers.org.nz

UK—www.alzheimers.org.uk/site/index.php

USA—www.nia.nih.gov/alzheimers

Bereavement

Australian Centre for Grief and Bereavement—www.grief.org. au/library_cat.html

Bereavement Care Centre, Australia—www.bereavementcare. com.au/index.htm

Cancer

Australia Cancer Council—free call 13 11 22, www.cancer council.com.au

CanTeen, Young Australians—www.canteen.org.au

NZ—Cancer Society of NZ, www.cancernz.org.nz

Planet Cancer, young adults with cancer—www.planetcancer. org/html/index.php

UK—Cancer UK, www.cancer-uk.org

USA National Cancer Institute—www.cancer.gov

Creative support

Amazions Sacred Arts—www.amazions.com.au

Grief to Memories: A workbook in life's significant losses —www.soras.com/books.htm

Depression

Beyond Blue—1300 22 4636, www.beyondblue.org.au

Salvos—13 72 58, 'Braver, Stronger, Wiser' DVD, www.salvos. org.au

Grief

Meditative movie—www.DoNotWeepMovie.com

Hospice support

Australia, Amitayus Hospice Service—(02) 6684 3808, www.amitayus.org.au

Australia—www.palliativecare.org.au

HOME Hospice, Australia—Australia-wide free call 1800 132 229, www.homehospice.com.au

International Association for Hospice & Palliative Care — www.hospicecare.com

NZ—www.hospice.org.nz

UK—www.ncpc.org.uk

USA—www.nhpco.org/templates/1/homepage.cfm

Natural/Ecological death

The Natural Death Centre, Australia—www.naturaldeath centre.org.au

The Natural Death Centre, UK—www.naturaldeath.org.uk

Suicide

Australian Institute for Suicide Research and Prevention—www. griffith.edu.au/health/australian-institute-suicide-research-prevention

Chris's suicide help page—www.geocities.com/HotSprings/ 1911

If you are thinking of suicide read this first—www.metanoia.
org/suicide

Our friend Joe—www.angelfire.com/ms/lindas/joe.html

Suicide.org, largest suicide prevention, awareness and support
website on the internet—www.suicide.org

Support for victims of crime, road and workplace incidents

Enough is Enough, Australia—www.enoughisenough.org.au

Homicide victims support group, Australia—www.hvsgnsw.
org.au

Homicide victims support group, global links—www.hvsgnsw.
org.au/links

'Out of Harm's Way' agreement—www.warringah.nsw.gov.au/
outofharmsway

Victim Services, Australia with global links—www.lawlink.nsw.
gov.au/vs

Victims of Crimes UK—www.voc.webeden.co.uk

VOCAL (Victims Of Crime Assistance League), Australia—
www.vocal.org.au

Workplace death—www.workplacedeath.wmb.org.au/support.
php

Acknowledgements

Our heartfelt gratitude goes to all our contributors who were prepared to revisit a place of loss and grief to tell their intimate stories. We are deeply indebted to them. They have shared their experiences so that others may find comfort and inspiration on their own journeys. To those whose stories weren't included in the book we are just as grateful; your experiences were no less powerful or deserving of sharing.

Very special thanks to our visionary publisher Maggie Hamilton, who has guided us with such passion and enthusiasm, and to Rosalind Price who introduced us; to Anne Deveson for her inspiring foreword; and to our wise and helpful editor Desney Shoemaker.

Thanks to Jennifer Lalor for her insights in 'Helping our children with grief'; to Chris Green, Alex and Aaron McShane, Julie Sutton, Greg Kirkham, Jenny Bathur, Sandra Lee, Fiona Williams and Kathy Stanwick for their wise words; and Elaine Seiler, Sabine and Vianney Pinon and Jennie Dell for their support.

Claire: My deep thanks go to Bobby Holcolm and my father John Waterson for showing me there was nothing to fear in death. My mother Valerie for her unconditional love and to my sister Roxana and my brother Merlin who have always been my sounding board and constant support. My daughters Carli and Tania whose love has encouraged me through the hard times, and to Lydia Duncan, Trish Clark, Iain Finlay and Andrew Watson, special mentors along the path. Enormous thanks to all my dear friends too numerous to mention by name, but you know who you are—you give meaning to my life. Finally, I honour the ancient wisdom of the many indigenous people who have shared their lives with me.

Trypheyna: Creation always involves the planting of a seed, and nothing grows in isolation. So it was with the seed Trish planted. She taught profound lessons and then left. Greg's love of Trish demonstrated in action the power of unconditional love. Theirs was an exquisite story waiting to be told. So the journey began. I owe immeasurable gratitude to my best friend and husband, Alex, whose faith and tireless support are priceless, to John and Liz, my parents, who shared their deaths with the same open hearts they lived their lives with, and our children Lorien, Azar, Aaron and Anastazia who embody grace and compassion.

Loving thanks to Giles and Nell Lynes, Joanna and Rex Howard, Greg Kirkham, Kristian McShane, Rhonda Richardson, Anne Owers, Richard White, Anne Deveson, David Wright, Catherine Camden-Pratt, Stuart Hill, Judy Pinn, Karen Bridgman, Graham Bird, Leonie Leonard, Karina and Frank Lucia, Vivienne, Johnnie, Tasman and Larna, The EE Team, Kate Hamilton, Chris Long, Diane Ann, Keith, Petrea King, Gerry Hellmrich, Judy Arpana, Eileen Jeboult, Ken and Lydia de la Motte, Greg Bell and Jenny Bathur, Lisa Sorensen, Alan Weinstein, Paul Walsh, Michael Brown, Indira Gail Charles, Della Walker, Gerard and Helen-Anne Manion, Melanie Greblo-Rhodes, and many others who shared their wisdom and love to make all this possible.

Zenith: My immense heartfelt gratitude goes to all those people who over the years have shared their deaths and their journeys with me. By wanting to embrace death and dying well, they have shown me what dying with grace looks like. A gift beyond price, and the way to go. They have enabled me to live my passion, learn on the job without too much pain, be of service and share this with others.

To Amitayus. To my truly amazing colleagues Joanne Doran and Nici Paitson. To HH the Dalai Lama, Thicht Nhat Hahn, Osho, Oneness and my other spiritual teachers and teachings, whose wisdom and guidance allowed and supported me to offer continuous support to others.

To my beloveds: Sylvia Morrow, Madeline Shaw, Margot Howard, Cheryl Williams, Kala Bodkin, Tamara Green, Bhajan Nickson, John Callanan and Jamie Dods. As well as all my other most wonderful, caring and loving friends, always there for me in so many ways. To my supportive community who wouldn't settle for less. Lastly to my three sons, Tane, Jodie and Tod, for just loving me against all the odds. We are all in it together.

Permissions

'My first baby dies at birth', adapted from the book *Layla's Story* by Vanessa Gorman, with kind permission of Penguin, Australia.

'My little boy sensed his death', adapted from *Mourning Has Broken: Learning from the wisdom of adversity* by Carmella B'Hahn, with kind permission of Crucible Publishers, Bath, UK.

'Contemplation of no coming and no going', *Chanting from the Heart* (2007) by Thicht Nhat Hahn, with kind permission of Parallex Press, Berkeley, California, USA.

(from left) Claire Leimbach, Trypheyna McShane and Zenith Virago.

About the authors

Claire Leimbach, photographer and writer, was commissioning editor for *Simply Living Magazine* and *Nature and Health*, as well as being a photojournalist with *Geo*. She has also worked on anthropological documentaries, and is fascinated by the amazing diversity of human cultures.

In her extensive travels among indigenous people she has witnessed the many different rituals surrounding death and dying. She came to realise this is one of the most important events in most cultures, and that there are countless ways in which death is both mourned and celebrated. She remains passionate about the plight of indigenous peoples and the environments in which they live.

Trypheyna McShane was brought up in West Africa, Denmark, England and the West Indies, arriving in Australia at the age of nineteen. As a mother, grandmother, artist, environmental educator and storyteller she sees links between the fear of death and damage to the earth. An international award-winning artist, her dream is to create an 'Eco Maze' on every continent. She has worked with Aboriginal communities, people with disabilities, young and old, and believes 'the arts' has solutions for ecological, economic, health and social issues.

Profoundly affected by the deaths of a number of people close to her, she collected stories on embracing death. Using creative practices, she encourages people to see how much there is to be grateful for.

Zenith Virago has pioneered a more holistic approach to death over fifteen years, while working with the dying and bereaved. As a professional death consultant, caretaker and celebrant she has a background in law and community work. She shares her extensive knowledge as a passionate educator, inspiring speaker and workshop leader with individuals, families, communities, hospice workers and other professionals.

Zenith is the founding member of the non-profit Natural Death Centre, Australia. She sees her work as a privilege and an important part of her life's journey, and it gives her a deep love and gratitude for the wonderful mystery of life and death of which we're all part.